SUSTAINABLE
AGRICULTURE
NETWORK
Handbook
Series
BOOK 2

STEEL IN THE FIELD

A Farmer's Guide to Weed Management Tools

EDITED BY GREG BOWMAN

A publication of the Sustainable Agriculture Network
with funding by the
Sustainable Agriculture Research and Education Program
of CSREES, U.S. Department of Agriculture

Sustainable Agriculture Network
National Agricultural Library
Beltsville, Maryland 20705-2351

Copyright ©1997 by the Sustainable Agriculture Network, with funding from the Sustainable Agriculture Research and Education program of the CSREES, U.S. Department of Agriculture. This study was supported in part by the funds of USDA, 94-COOP-1-0515.

SAN, the national outreach partner of the USDA-SARE program, is a consortium of individuals, universities and government, business and nonprofit organizations dedicated to the exchange of information on sustainable agricultural systems.

For more information about the Sustainable Agriculture Network, or about other SAN publications, contact:

Andy Clark
SAN Coordinator
c/o AFSIC, Room 304
National Agricultural Library
10301 Baltimore Avenue
Beltsville, MD 20705-2351
PH: (301)504-6425
FAX: (301)504-6409
san@nal.usda.gov

SARE is a competitive grants program. It provides funding for research and education projects that promote agricultural systems that are profitable, environmentally sound and enhance the viability of rural communities nationwide.

For more information about the SARE program and SARE grants contact:

Office of Sustainable Agriculture Programs
U.S. Department of Agriculture
1400 Independence Ave., S.W., Stop 2223
Washington, D.C. 20250-2223

Material for this book and its covers was researched, written, illustrated, edited and produced by the Rodale Institute, Kutztown, Pa. The book concept, format, and selection of featured farmers and content reviewers were developed under the auspices of the Sustainable Agriculture Network.

To order copies of this book, call (802)656-0471, or send a check or purchase order for $18.00 to:

Sustainable Agriculture Publications
Hills Building
University of Vermont
Burlington VT 05405-0082
nesare@zoo.uvm.edu

Please be sure to include your mailing address and telephone number.

The Sustainable Agriculture Network Handbook Series previous titles include Book 1: *Managing Cover Crops Profitably*, edited by the staff of the Rodale Institute.

Library of Congress Cataloguing-in-Publication Data

Steel in the field : a farmer's guide to
    weed management tools /
    edited by Greg Bowman.
            p.   cm. — (Sustainable Agriculture
    Network handbook series ; 2)
        Includes bibliographical references and index.
        ISBN 1-888626-02-X (alk. paper : soft cover)
        1. Agricultural implements. 2. Weeds—Control.
    I. Bowman, Greg, 1952-   . II. Series.
    S676.S69   1997
    681'.7631—dc21   97-8406
                                                 CIP

2   4   6   8   9   7   5   3   1

Printed in the United States of America on recycled paper ♻

The USDA-SARE program provides information to everyone, without regard to race, religion, national origin, sex, age, disability, familial or veteran status.

Every effort has been made to make this book as complete and as accurate as possible and to educate the reader. This text is only a guide, however, and should be used in conjunction with other information sources on weed-, herbicide-, and farm management. No single tool or weed control strategy will be appropriate and effective for all conditions. The editor/authors and publisher disclaim any liability, loss, or risk, personal or otherwise, which is incurred as a consequence, directly or indirectly, of the use and application of any of the contents of this book.

Mention, visual representation or inferred reference of a product, service, manufacturer or organization in this publication does not imply endorsement by the USDA, the SARE program or the authors. Exclusion does not imply a negative evaluation.

Graphic design, interior layout and cover type design: Jerry O'Brien. All interior illustrations: John Gist. Cover illustration: Franklin Fretz. Farmer narratives on Rich Bennett and Jack Erisman written by Christopher Shirley. All others by Greg Bowman. Text Editing: Craig Cramer. Copy Editing: Cheryl Lachowski. Indexing: Manuscript Doctors (Nancy Hopkins).

Acknowledgments

Dairy farmer John Merrill's frustration with trying to find a rotary hoe—and someone anywhere close to New England who knew how to operate one—was the origin of this book. He shared this information hole with his colleagues on a committee of the Sustainable Agriculture Research and Education (SARE) program. Like many other SARE groups, this committee was a cross-section of farmers, educators, researchers and farm specialists. They agreed that farmers needed a nuts and bolts book on how to find and use weed management tools profitably and sustainably.

Beth Holtzman, communications specialist for the Northeast Region SARE program, and Fred Magdoff, coordinator of SARE's Northeast Region, developed the question into a concept. Both individuals were patient and supportive in seeing this project through.

I repeatedly interviewed the farmers who are featured in this book. Each gave generously of his time, experience and on-farm research findings, formal or informal. These innovators are the real authors of this book. Many frequently open their farms to other members of regional sustainable farming networks where real farmer-to-farmer exchange takes place.

Providing unfailing good sense was Dale Kumpf of Fleischer Manufacturing. He knows farmers throughout the U.S. and Mexico who are familiar enough with their farms to know when steel is ideal. Richard R. Johnson and Al Higley at Deere and Company—and the dozens of Deere specialists they linked me to at the right moments—provided images, specifications, insight, statistics and technical explanations that could only come from a world-class corporation. Ralph Moore of Market Farm Implement, Somerset, Pa., shared repeatedly of his deep working knowledge of horticultural tools, as he does daily with farmers across the U.S.

Vern Grubinger at the University of Vermont recommended farmer contacts and tools. Richard Parish, Dan Ball and Thomas Lanini at the state universities of Louisiana, Oregon and California at Davis, respectively, provided important perspective on crops, tools and farmers in their regions. I frequently consulted Rick Exner of the Practical Farmers of Iowa.

Helping to distill and express all this shared wisdom was Craig Cramer, who has yet to see a sustainable farming sentence he couldn't improve. He and the reviewers listed at the back of the book immensely enhanced this effort. Errors that remain are mine. These individuals lent their expertise without compensation simply to make this book as valuable as possible to the people who choose to make sustainable farming work in these United States.

To all these and many others, many thanks.

Greg Bowman
Kutztown, Pa.
January, 1997

Publisher's Foreword

Controlling weeds with reduced reliance on herbicides is one of the main challenges facing farmers interested in moving towards a more sustainable agriculture. There are many reasons farmers are moving away from complete reliance on herbicides. Health concerns of those handling herbicides and concern with groundwater contamination are among them. However, the development of weeds that are resistant to commonly used herbicides and the high costs of bringing less environmentally harmful herbicides to market have made finding alternative weed control strategies of great practical importance.

There are many techniques for weed control, including good selection of crop sequences in the rotation, the use of cover crops to compete with and smother weeds, and mechanical cultivation.

In some ways, cultivation for weed control is almost a lost art. Herbicides seemed to work so well for so long that many farmers abandoned mechanical means of control. But now there are new implements and improved versions of the basic rotary hoes, basket weeders, and flame weeders of 50 years ago.

The goal of this book is to provide you with information about how each implement works in the field and in sustainable weed management systems. Not only that, it also explains under what conditions a tool is the most useful, what problems other farmers have found using it and where can you get more information about it.

You may want to travel to farms or research sites to see some of these implements in use. Our hope is that this book will help reduce the legwork in finding the right set of implements for your operation.

Got any hot tips for us? We would be *very* interested in your suggestions for other publications or videos that would help you farm more sustainably. Also, we would really appreciate your thoughts about the content and format of this book.

After you have spent time with the book, please fill out and send the enclosed self-mailer evaluation sheet in the back. This will help us provide better information to you in the future.

Fred Magdoff
Regional Coordinator, Northeast SARE Program
Sustainable Agriculture Network
University of Vermont
January 1997

Contents

Cultivation in Context:
Renewed tools for better farming

Spend less. Manage more. Take control.

Here's a deal for you. Invest in a few pieces of well-chosen steel, diversify your crop mix for higher-value marketing, and harvest a higher return to your bottom line through big savings on herbicide.

Interested? I thought so.

Keep in mind, whether you farm 1 acre or 1,000 acres, you can save in many ways—not just in dollars and cents. The tools and techniques you read about in this book will also pay off in less liability, greater management flexibility, less trouble with herbicide-resistant weeds and reduced off-farm environmental impacts.

Thinking about weed control changed dramatically in the years following World War II. Scientists working for the Allies developed growth-regulating compounds known today as 2,4-D and MCDA. When these chemicals "leaked" into the biological research community, it soon became clear they could be formulated to kill broadleaf weeds and not harm corn. These herbicides helped to reduce the need for cultivation and led to greater plant populations per acre. Check planting in wide rows of aligned hills (to allow cultivating across rows) gave way to drilled corn in narrower rows.

Herbicides, affordable hybrid corn seed and inexpensive nitrogen fertilizers opened new production frontiers throughout the '50s. The arrival in the '60s of atrazine and other herbicides that provided control for a wide range of weeds led to the wholesale abandonment of mechanical weed control (MWC) in some areas.

Tough-to-mount and painfully-boring-to-operate cultivators frequently became fencerow architecture. Farm-country cultivating skills and wisdom dwindled as herbicides simplified decision-making. Researchers can trace the origin of herbicide-resistant weeds, as well as "new" weeds, to the very areas where cultivation ceased.

However, mechanical weed control is still important to many farmers. While national aggregate sales of cultivating equipment slowly declined through the '80s and '90s, use of cultivators remains fairly common in scattered areas. Many farmers cultivate in some row-cropping regions of the Midwest and South. Vegetable farmers, especially in California, keep farmshop welders at work creating custom tools that fit their specialized needs. And ridge-till farming (see page 34) usually means at least an annual ridge-forming cultivator pass.

The current interest in mechanical and flame weed control tools as a preferred technology began long ago with farmers who decided—for a range of reasons—not to abandon their "steel" for herbicides. A few individuals never switched. Many contemporary tool users blend physical and chemical weed management modes. Some depend primarily on mechanical controls, using partial rates or "banding" herbicide in a swath just over the row area. Others use full broadcast rates and continue to cultivate to ensure top yields—or just because it feels right.

While the "other-than-herbicide" group of farmers has grown significantly in the past 30 years, it is still a distinct minority. Yet, out of necessity, these farmers have preserved weed management skills and developed sophisticated tools to produce crops profitably.

Steel used appropriately can cut herbicide costs. But an integrated mechanical tool approach wins in other ways, too. It deals effectively with herbicide-resistant weeds, perennial weeds in no-till fields, and soil types that respond positively to occasional tillage within a no-till system. Mixing in the optimum combination of tools and cultural weed management preserves the effectiveness of herbicides through limiting their use. When farmers bring together *improved* tools with all these factors, many find that an integrated, steel-based approach is their least risky, most profitable option.

There are even signs of a watershed in how mainline agricultural researchers will view the weed control future. Orvin C. Burnside is a veteran weed scientist at the University of Minnesota. In 1993, he authored a perspective piece titled "Weed Science—The Step Child" (*Weed Technology,* Vol. 7, Issue 2, pp. 515-518). He wrote

> Public weed scientists need to undertake a "crash program" to develop alternative weed control technologies that will be needed if herbicide use is reduced because of the economics of weed management, public concern, or government regulation. There needs to be a paradigm shift away from over dependence on herbicides that presently are our primary weapons in weed control.

Later, Burnside called for a systems approach using preventive, mechanical, cultural, biological, chemical and integrated strategies in his address to the North Central Weed Science Society's 1995 annual meeting.

If these professionals pursue research into biological and mechanical strategies as aggressively as they have herbicides, many farmers featured in this book are ready to help. These visionary, self-funded agriculturists have practical, farm-tested techniques to share and plenty of new ideas to test and refine.

Expectations of tillage have changed dramatically in 50 years. Farmers are under critical scrutiny from their neighbors and regulators to keep streams clean and topsoil in place. Yet, as they devote more management to meet rising environmental standards, farmers wonder how to find new ways to make their operation profitable.

To win acceptance in the '90s by farmers who know it only by its negative reputation, mechanical weed control has to show it can meet these challenges. This strategy has its own demands and limits, but also offers its own assurances. Through market incentives or crop diversification options, some operators decide that the benefits of not using herbicides justify the trade-off of mastering broader management skills. Other operators see well-managed herbicides and steel tools as equally useful and acceptable, and invest in learning how to fine-tine the combination.

Facing the Questions

Sure, steel and flame tools can kill weeds. But can they become the foundation of a weed management strategy that works profitably across a range of conditions?

Inevitably, those new to mechanical weed control will ask some of these questions:
- Is it economically efficient?
- Is it as effective as herbicides?
- Is it dependable?
- Is it unwise, because of soil erosion, moisture loss or increased compaction?

The answers must be considered in light of each farmer's "big picture" approach to crop and soil management. No single tool will provide season-long, year-in/year-out success. But the same is true for herbicides. An appropriate selection of weed management implements can succeed as part of an integrated system with two fundamental requirements: **weed competition is suppressed and rows are straight.**

CULTIVATION PAYS WELL

Farmer Ron Rosmann of Harlan, Iowa, works with the Iowa State University "weed team" of agricultural specialists. About his experience with an aggressive, high-residue cultivator and an electro-hydraulic guidance system, he says: "Over 14 years, assuming herbicide costs at $20/acre, after subtracting a $20,000 investment in cultivation equipment, I've saved $70,000 on herbicides. Look how long that initial investment can work for you, compared to herbicides you have to apply every year. ...Some bigger farmers think they don't have time to cultivate, but it's the net return that they should be looking at." ("Harlan farmer considers cultivation critical," by Elizabeth Weber, editor, *Leopold Letter,* Leopold Center for Sustainable Agriculture, Vol. 8, Number 4, Winter 1996, (515) 294-3711.)

Managing overall weed pressure includes making this year's crop more competitive against weeds and preventing weed seeds or reproductive tissue from building up in the soil. "Cultural management" steps of crop production include crop rotation, the timing of planting, the soil's biological health and soil physical quality, cover crops (varied rooting depth and soil environment), variety selection, and crop spacing to outcompete weeds.

Some growers achieve uniformly parallel rows with a traditional row-marker disk on an outrigger arm on their planter, while others turn to some type of guidance system. Consistent row alignment allows close-to-the-row settings and high speed. Straight rows and guidance systems change the whole economic picture of mechanical weed control—and how the driver feels by evening. They greatly increase how many acres per day your cultivator can cover, without increasing labor or cultivator costs. Close cultivation decreases how wide the herbicide band needs to be, and allows crop canopy to shade out weeds sooner in the season. Speed makes it easier to throw weed-smothering soil into the rows during late-season passes.

So, how about MWC—with straight rows and a handle on weed pressure—compared with current herbicide-only systems?

Is MWC economically efficient?

In the Corn Belt, annual herbicide costs (material, application and labor) in 1996 were in the area of $20 to $25 per acre for corn and $25 to $30 per acre for soybeans. An all-mechanical, no-herbicide approach might take two rotary hoeings (at about $2 each) and two cultivations (at about $4 each for a 6R30 unit—one covering six rows, 30 inches apart). That's $12 per acre, figured at $9.25 per hour for labor.

That total jumps to $22 per acre in dryland, contoured grain sorghum. Further, the "opportunity cost" of labor in critical times varies greatly.

Cost per acre also varies by scale. Agronomists at the University of Wisconsin estimated in 1990 that it cost $3.30 per acre for a farmer to rotary hoe once if the farmer had 100 acres of row crops, but only $1.65 if the farmer had 500 acres.

In mechanical and chemical systems, efficiency varies with weather, planting, crop conditions and the skill of the farmer. An emergency mechanical or herbicide "rescue treatment" can be significant. The unplanned trip will be efficient if it costs less than the yield loss that weeds would have caused.

A mixed approach holds the most promise for the most growers. Banding herbicides places the chemical in a limited-width strip over the row, usually 10 to 15 inches wide. A single herbicide application, banded preemergence, followed by a single late-season cultivation, can manage weeds as effectively as broadcast herbicide-only and with less than half the material, for less money and with reduced herbicide exposure to humans and the environment.

That's the assertion of Mark Hanna, an Iowa State University agricultural and biosystems engineer who led a four-year study. He says the mix would save an average of $9 per acre for Iowa corn growers, and should apply to wide-row soybeans as well. ("No-till study offers new incentive to cultivate," *Leopold Letter,* Vol. 8, No. 4, Winter 1996, Leopold Center for Sustainable Agriculture.)

In fields with moderate to heavy weed pressure with 10-inch herbicide bands, watch weed pressure closely. An earlier, additional cultivation may be needed to keep the crop competitive.

Dairy operators face excruciating labor demands at first cultivation because of haying. Ways to stretch out the cultivation window include staggered plantings of corn and soybeans to prevent large blocks from being ready at once, and diversifying into small grain or vegetable crops to further spread out the work load.

Is MWC effective at controlling weeds?

How about in-row weeds and escapes in the "guess-row" area between planter passes?

MWC must be part of a weed management system. Because it deals with biological observation, crop stages and implement adjustments, mechanical weed control is an acquired skill. Farmers say it is art *and* science. They report that effectiveness of an integrated, mechanical-based weed strategy increases over time. Sustainable soil management brings gradual improvements year to year, and farmers learn new techniques.

The total effect becomes greater than the sum of the parts—fewer weeds in more mellow soil are out-maneuvered by synchronized crop rotations and disrupted by more expertly applied tillage or flaming. Close attention to fertility balance to lessen deficiencies and excesses gives crops more advantage. Narrower rows and precision seed placement increase the canopy effect.

In-row weeds deserve particular attention. Start early if you want to win. Management steps that hold weeds back in the days just after planting give crops a competitive advantage. When the crop is large enough to withstand soil flow, tools that move soil into the row can smother small, in-row weeds. This requires soil that "flows" and rows straight enough to keep cultivation speed high. Specialized in-row weeding tools developed originally for vegetables actually move between crop plants.

Is MWC dependable?

Wet fields, dry fields and schedule conflicts can hobble any weed control program. More options cover more contingencies. Sometimes cultivation can rescue a failed herbicide treatment. Other times a spot spray or postemergent herbicide pass can save a crop that remains too wet to cultivate.

Experienced farmers committed to mechanical weed control report they are no more vulnerable to **economic losses** from weeds than their neighbors with well managed herbicide programs. Some years they even fare better, but they would have a harder time guaranteeing a cosmetically perfect field, year after year.

Having the tool and labor capacity to cover crop acres within tight windows is a matter of weighing the odds then making a choice. Keep careful records on acres per day per tool and on hours per field. Figure the total time required compared with your average weather window. Scaling up tool capacity has to be a part of taking on more acres of the same crop with similar planting dates. Sequencing planting dates or changing crops are other options.

Wet years will come, but they don't have to doom mechanical controls. Once you decide how small a cultivation time window you're willing to work in, line up tools and drivers for the critical times. Emergency decisions are eased if you know the limits of your tools and the relative costs of weed-induced production losses. Marketing plans, weed characteristics and alternate crop use all play a part.

Is it unwise?

What about soil erosion, moisture loss or increased compaction?

Poorly managed tillage can cause these problems, as well as waste fossil fuel and harm crop growth. Mistakes include using the wrong tool or using the right tool at the wrong time, too often, in the wrong way, in the wrong place or at an improper orientation to field slope.

The general rule for MWC tillage is that it be as **shallow**, as **infrequent**, as **specific to the weed** problem, and as **limited in soil impact** as possible. Where following these guidelines still results in muddy water, dry root zones, damaged crop roots or compacted row areas, MWC is not appropriate as applied. You may seek assistance from an individual in your region or specialty from the "Contacts" list on page 118.

You make the difference by selecting the right tool and using it wisely. Occasional tillage—even moldboard plowing done properly—can actually decrease erosion by increasing moisture infiltration rates.

Cover crops, compost, manure and other organic matter incorporated into biologically active soil bring measurable changes. Properly managed, additional organic matter can increase infiltration and water-holding capacity, thereby reducing erosion potential.

A cultivation pass before a rain shower will have less impact where soil has greater tilth and soaks up more water. The same tool used the same way across the road on "tighter" soil will create channels and probably lead to more erosive water movement.

Where soil moisture is usually marginal, soil and residue disturbances should be minimized. Local soil types, precipitation patterns and crop systems give specialized weeding tools a role. Cases include shattering the soil crust after planting but before crop emergence, or intentionally creating a slightly compacted zone just under the soil surface to retain moisture.

A controlled traffic field plan (running equipment wheels in the same row middles season to season), using deep-rooted rotation crops and staying out of the field in wet conditions help to minimize compaction.

Maximizing The Benefits

MWC that works offers clear advantages for sustainable farming. These include four opportunities.

Develop weed control customized to your farm. Remember, tools are only part of a site-specific, self-sufficient system. Their highest use comes mixed with years of on-farm observation of your soils, crops and weather. Start where you are, learning from other farmers with related tools, crops, soils, weeds and farming goals. As you work with more of these variables, your system becomes more flexible and more adapted to your farm—in sum, more site-specific and more sustainable.

Reduce annual expense for consumable purchased inputs. Yearly costs for herbicides can be reduced as tool use increases. Most weed tools work years after they're paid for. Spray equipment does, too. Herbicides you buy every growing season.

Reasonable maintenance and appropriate use lets you run cultivators for many seasons. Sweep wear is gauged in thousands of acres, with replaceable blades minimizing the new steel needed for a clean cut. Moving parts in some weed tools increase soil action as well as maintenance needs, but still give long service.

Mesh weed management with crop rotation and soil tilth improvement. Tillage that replaces herbicides uncouples crop selection from any limits of chemical carryover. This freedom maximizes cropping opportunities. It increases options when you are re-planting an alternative crop in the event of a crop failure or a weather catastrophe. You can interplant crops or use narrow-strip tillage of several crops without concern about herbicide drift causing damage.

Adding small grains or forage crops to a rotation reduces the size of the niche for annual weeds by shifting the seasonal opening for weed growth. Plus these crops can add biomass to the soil when residue is unharvested. Pre-plant tillage can serve dual purposes of incorporating covers and preparing a seed bed. Rotating warm- and cool season crops is another way to put weeds on the defensive.

Innovative farmers are exploring no-till planting into cover crops left on the surface. These operators use chemical or mechanical means to kill covers, then plant seed or vegetable transplants with tools that create openings just big enough for the job. This route suppresses weeds, preserves moisture and creates habitat for beneficial insects. Carefully incorporating sufficient cover crops with tillage can significantly improve soil water retention, which reduces surface run off with its erosive tendency. Extra organic matter added over time also increases a soil's tendency to flow better when tilled because it becomes more granular and less cloddy. Covers can suck up moisture as they mature, which can be a problem in dry years.

Profit from new, high-value markets for non-chemically produced crops. A MWC-based, non-herbicide system often offers relief from pesticide applicator's licensing; incurring new environmental liability from chemical surface runoff, groundwater contamination or spray drift; health risks to applicators or family members; and any accidental contact with livestock or non-target crops.

Opportunities are increasing for food crops grown under more ecologically sustainable management. More buyers—local, regional and national—pay premium prices for vegetables, fruits and grains grown under Integrated Pest Management systems, or even from fields that receive no herbicides for the current cropping season. Organic dairies need grains and hay—and prefer them to be regionally grown. Exporters need high quality, specially grown grains and soybeans for customers in Europe and Japan. Local food buyers, from families to restaurants, seek out vegetables, grains and livestock raised in ways that seem to be more ecologically safe.

Even without a market that rewards a shift to lower pesticide use, you gain a positive conversation starter with consumers and neighbors. You have new chances to win support for your farming operation from local non-farmers interested in environmental issues. Explain the alternative measures you're taking to produce profitable crops. Highlight the extra effort you give to understanding your farm's complex ecological balance.

Every farmer has a unique range of skills, economic situations and natural resources. Choosing the most sustainable mix—for weed management and for an overall, whole-farm approach—is a privilege and a responsibility that should stay as close to home as possible. When your tools fit your system, you're the one in charge.

ABCs of mechanical and cultural weed management

In a sustainable farm plan, each type of implement is only one part of a long-term weed management strategy. Any tool will disappoint when it's asked to do more than it was designed to do. A successful strategy distributes weed-limiting and weed-killing roles into complementary parts. The benefits of crop diversity and soil improvements in lowering weed pressure increase over time. This trend lessens the economic hit when weed control steps face difficulty.

Critical principles of sustainable, integrated weed control using steel or flame include

A. Give the crop the advantage.
Steel tools succeed best when you focus on weed prevention, lessening the vigor and number of weeds that need to be killed. Delayed planting is a key here. Crops germinate quicker in warmer soil. They spend fewer days in the ground before they begin to outgrow weeds or form a shady canopy that sets back weeds.

Intensive, early season weeding is a second distinguishing feature of a system based on mechanical weed control (MWC). It keeps crops ahead by hitting weeds as soon after germination as possible—long before they are a physical threat to the crop. Causing weeds to die by physical means (tearing, cutting, root drying or flaming) is much easier and more efficient when the weeds are tiny and vulnerable. By the time they threaten the crop with shading and competition for soil moisture and fertility, they are much more difficult to kill with cultivation. Postemergent herbicide application gives a little more leeway.

B. Keep weeds on the defensive.
Weed seeds wait each spring for heat and light to induce germination. Don't wake them up unless you have a way to take them out.

Several farmers in this book describe their version of a "stale seedbed." (See stories about Jim Cavin, Rich de Wilde, Carmen Fernholz and Paul Muller.) They do one or two shallow tillage passes to stimulate germination of surface weed seeds before crop-planting time. Irrigation or warm, moist soil conditions spur weed seed germination that triggers a control pass with tillage or flame. By minimizing subsequent tillage at planting that would stimulate new weed seeds, the crop comes up through pre-weeded soil.

Any planter can be less of a weed-helper if it is tooled to leave soil as loose as possible over the seed row, while still creating good seed-soil contact. Packer wheels at the surface press light-stimulated weed seeds into moisture. Ridge-till planters move fresh weed seed from the rows by skimming the top inch or so of topsoil from the row to the middles, where cultivators can attack weeds more easily.

Your crops can out-compete weeds through well-planned crop rotations. Manage the crop sequence to minimize ecological openings for weeds. Mix crop rooting depth, root type (taprooted or fibrous), and seasonal surface cover. Vary the timing and depth of tillage. In mature, sophisticated rotations, crops emerge in ideal conditions while weeds struggle to find an opening to survive.

C. Accept weeds that don't really matter.
Separate how you *feel* about weeds in your fields from their potential to diminish production. Agronomically, weeds are an economic problem only if they decrease yield—now or in the future—by more than the cost of managing them. If the aesthetics of a clean field are important, you need to be honest about the extra cost.

Weed species vary in how much of a threat they pose to crop vigor. Some winter annuals provide soil protection. Some annual weeds in forage crops provide nutrition for livestock or abundant residue to build soil. Weeds that don't go to seed in a cover-crop stand count as biomass to soil microbes and warrant only your watchful eye.

"Eradication of all weeds is a virtual ring in the nose of farmers," claims organic farmer Terry Jacobson of Wales, ND. That goal can tempt farmers to over-control with chemicals or excess tillage, he says.

Jacobson wants to learn more each season about weeds. He wants to know which ones he can live with, which ones are worth containing and which ones are telling him where he needs to make improvements in crop or soil management. ∎

How to Use This Book

A single tool can be used in many ways. So don't be limited by this book's presentation of tools in three general sections by cropping system:

Agronomic row crop tools (for corn, soybeans, grain sorghum and cotton) include broadcast tillage implements for early weed control, and tools that work between the rows as crops mature.

Horticultural crop tools include implements for bedded vegetables and for in-row weeding between plants or trees.

Dryland crop tools control weeds efficiently in vast fields while managing residue and conserving moisture during the fallow times between cropping periods.

Each section has two parts: **"The Tools"** (technical information on each of its featured tools) followed by **"The Farmers"** (narratives illustrating how farmers fit tools to their conditions).

The technical sections, outlined in detail below, feature drawings of important design elements. You learn here—at a glance—the *facts* of the tool. In their narratives, farmers explain how they integrate tools with the other parts of their weed management system—planting time, soil building, crop rotation and tillage mode. They provide you with the rest of the story—the *art* of the tool. Selecting the right technology is only part of the equation. A tool's wise use and adaptation to each farm are at least as important in making it part of a sustainable system.

The Tools

Two **bar graphs** begin the full-page entries. The top bar shows the estimated crop height range where the tool is most effective. The lower bar shows the estimated height range of weeds that the tool can handle.

The intensity of shading within the bars indicates the degree of certainty of the recommendation, i.e. the darker the shading, the more sure the effect. *These are general guides reflecting a range of experiences. Actual effectiveness will vary according to your conditions and operating methods.*

A tool **overview** summarizes how a tool works, its roles and important applications for weed management.

In **design features,** the mechanical and engineering highlights of the tool's shape, components and features are detailed.

Under **model for comparison** is a particular size of the tool—in some cases specifically outfitted—that is used for price comparison between makers. The 1996 list price figures were submitted by participating sources who also provided average PTO horsepower and field operating speed.

Width range, all makers/all models shows the widest and narrowest of all versions of a tool offered. **Sources** lists the reference number of commercial contacts found in "Tool Sources" at the rear of the book. **Farmers** shows where to find the tool described in a farm narrative. Some tools were not used by any of the interviewed farmers.

The Farmers

Each farmer's narrative opens with general information about farm size, crops, soils, tillage style and cropping systems. **Weed management highlights** show the cultural steps and the tools used by the farmer. **Boldface type** highlights each farmer's first description of a tool that is illustrated in the Technical Section.

The Toolshed

Farmer sidebars add details to the narratives. **Reviewers** lists experts whose advice improved this book. The **Glossary** provides working definitions for tool-related terms. **Horticultural tool sources** includes contact information for specialty tractors suitable for cultivating (high clearance, offset fuselage, rear motor, light frame). **Publications and information** tells you how to learn more. **Contacts** gives ways to reach individuals willing to share of their knowledge.

Tool Sources is a numbered listing of tool manufacturers, North American distributors of foreign tools, and regional suppliers. The index lists tool text references, tool illustrations, farmers, tool parts, weeds varieties, tillage modes and cropping practices. ■

I. Agronomic Row Crops

The Tools

A flexible combination of tools, timing and technique to suppress early season weeds is the foundation of an integrated row-crop weed management program. Broadcast weeding tools, used in conjunction with cover crops and primary tillage, offer an alternative to herbicides at planting to control weed competition.

Rotary hoes, flex-tine weeders, spike-tooth harrows and rolling bar baskets all provide shallow, thorough stirring of the soil that kills sprouting and emerging weeds the full width of the tool. The action knocks soil from weed roots, causing them to die. Control is best when field conditions are hot, dry and sunny.

Flame weeding just prior to and just after crop emergence is also effective in establishing early control in some crops. Of the entire group of broadcast tillage or flaming tools, only specially designed rotary hoes work well in fields with appreciable crop residue.

Post-plant treatment for weed control *before crop emergence* is a delicate, time sensitive maneuver. It depends on the ability of an implement to kill surface weeds without mortally disturbing the germinating crop. For pre-emergent treatments to be effective, the crop must be planted deeper than the working depth of the broadcast tillage tool. Postemergence, the crop must be more firmly rooted than competing weeds to survive the weeding pass.

Years of crusted spring soils boost rotary hoe sales. In these times, the tool's flicking and shattering of soil particles to kill weeds takes second place to its ability to aerate a rain-packed soil surface. Extra weight helps crust penetration but makes gauge wheels a necessity. A pair of these supporting tires, one under either side of the rotary hoe toolbar, maintains even penetration by the hoe points. On rough fields, the tires prevent gouging by the hoe wheels on one end of the toolbar.

Rotary hoes are not good weeders in tilthy, soft soils. In these conditions, the dragging action of soil-stirring harrows and tine weeders tend to be more effective.

The rotary hoe is an effective and efficient tool within a sharply limited window of weed size. Once weeds form true leaves or you can see them while driving by from your tractor seat, many will survive. Doubling back to cover the same field a second time—in the same or opposite direction immediately, or in several days when re-rooting of weeds begins—often boosts effectiveness if weed pressure is strong, residue interferes, or cloudy, humid conditions slow weed kill.

Crops at large vary in their tolerance of rotary hoeing, with species having a strong but flexible center stem surviving best. Row crops—and even tomatoes—can survive rotary hoeing at 8 to 12 inches tall if an emergency pass is needed to control small weeds before a cultivator is available.

Note: This book presents tools in three categories by crop type where they are commonly used. Many tools are employed effectively in diverse systems. The farmer narratives show how the same tool works well in different crops and for different purposes.

Standard Rotary Hoe

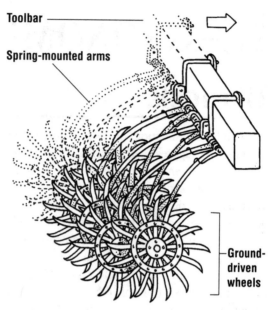

Toolbar

Spring-mounted arms

Ground-driven wheels

CROP height range estimate (must be large-seeded)

			CORN							
			SOYBEANS							
0"	2"	4"	6"	8"	10"	12"	18"	24"	30"	36"

WEED height range (annuals) estimate

■ suitable   ■ less suitable   ☐ unsuitable

Match tillage timing, depth and location to crop root growth. Weed control varies with soil conditions and weed density.

Overview: In clean-tilled or low-residue fields, the sharp-edged, rounded teeth on rotary hoe spokes aggressively uproot weeds in the pre-emergent, white-root stage. Hoes work before or after crops are up, as long as crop seed is more deeply rooted than weeds and crop tissue damage is not too severe. Rotary hoes are used for "broadcast" cultivation, i.e. lightly tilling their full width at 1" to 2" deep without regard to crop rows. Faster speed enhances surface aggressiveness but decreases penetration. Rotary hoes have a vertical entrance and surface shattering action ideal for aerating crusted soils. Increase corn seeding rate about 2 percent per intended mechanical pass to compensate for possible plant population reductions.

Design Features: Curved steel spokes radiating as a flat wheel from a hub are rotated forward by ground contact. The curvature accelerates the exit of a tooth tip from the soil, sharply kicking up soil and weeds. Rigid or folding toolbar; 18" to 21" wheels; 16 teeth per wheel; wheels on 3.5" centers. One or two wheels per arm, with most models using down-pressure springs for consistent penetration on uneven surfaces. **Cautions:** worn tips greatly decrease effectiveness. Replace worn hub bearings as needed for smooth operation. Bolt attachments, rather than rivets, makes bearing replacement easier. Residue, corn rootballs, stones, sticks and plastic can plug wheels. Adding knives to cut residue or increasing spacing between wheels can improve performance in these conditions. (See next page.)

Options: Gauge wheels (recommended); extra down-pressure springs for crusted soil. (Other options for extending hoe use are described on the next page.)

▶ **Model for comparison:** 21', rigid-frame
  Rec. PTO HP: 75 to 90   **Speed:** 5 to 15 mph   **List price:** $4,000 to $5,600 ($4,643 avg.)
Width range (all makers/all models): 10' to 42'

Sources: 18, 26, 47, 62, 81, 105
Farmers: Berning, Cavin, de Wilde, Fernholz, Kenagy, McKaskle, Spray

TIPS: Don't hoe bean crops from the brittle "crook" stage to three days later. Don't expect a rotary hoe to kill green weeds—they've usually developed too deep a root system.

High-Residue Rotary Hoe

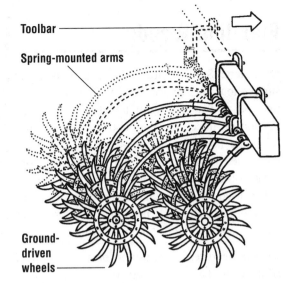

Toolbar

Spring-mounted arms

Ground-driven wheels

Working ranges same as for standard hoe

Overview: Same operating principles as standard rotary hoe (previous entry), but works in fields with up to 60 percent residue *as long as teeth still are able to penetrate into the soil surface.* Optional knives and spacers help to cut residue and reduce plugging. (See below.)

Design Features: Greater clearance for residue flow than standard hoe; built with more distance between front and rear wheels as well as between the toolbar and soil surface. Wheels are self-cleaning.

▶ **Model for comparison:** 21', rigid-frame
Rec. PTO HP: 80 to 100   **Speed:** 5 to 15 mph   **List price:** $4,850 to $5,750 ($5,184 avg.)

Width range (all makers/all models): 15' to 41'

Sources: 47, 62, 105   **Farmers:** Erisman, Thacker, Thompson

Rotary Hoe Accessories

Bearing Protector and Residue-Knife Kit

Overview: An insert extends the wheel axle, moving each wheel closer to the adjoining arm where two stationary sickle-bar mower blades shred residue brought up by wheels.

Hoe arm

Blades

Insert

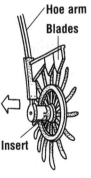

Design Features: Allows hoeing in heavier residue.

Price: $17 to $25 for bearing protectors, $4 to $8 for knife kits (Deere units higher).

Source: 42

Replacement Tooth Tips

Overview: Weld-on "spoons" restore aggressive soil penetration after original teeth wear down.

Design Features: Rolled steel: 0.75" wide, 0.12" thick, and 2.37" long. Weld freehand or with jigs.

Price: $0.75 per spoon ($12 per wheel). Production welding jig, $100.

Source: 64

Farmer: Spray

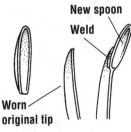

New spoon

Weld

Worn original tip

Extender Arms (for Deere Rotary Hoes)

Overview: Doubles rocker-arm length to improve residue flow, allowing operation in heavier residue.

Design Features: Sets wheels so that wheels self-clean.

Price: $7.75 per arm, about $14 per toolbar foot.   **Source:** 86

Flex-tine Weeder

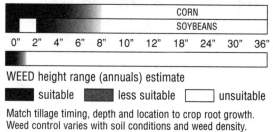

CROP height range estimate

							CORN			
					SOYBEANS					
0"	2"	4"	6"	8"	10"	12"	18"	24"	30"	36"

WEED height range (annuals) estimate

⬛ suitable   ⬛ less suitable   ☐ unsuitable

Match tillage timing, depth and location to crop root growth.
Weed control varies with soil conditions and weed density.

Overview: Spring wire tines scratch the soil surface to uproot tiny weed seedlings. Up to 25 tines per toolbar foot are mounted in a staggered fashion on three or six mounting bars, resembling the layout of a spike-tooth harrow. The bent tines vibrate rapidly and glide around or over obstructions. A tine weeder works in loose or lightly crusted soil with no long-stemmed residue. When used postemergence, crops must be well-rooted. Excellent within its limits for high speed, preemergence and early postemergence broadcast weeding. Stiffer tines break through heavier crusts but lose some of their vibrating action.

Design Features: Coiled-loop or other spring mounting may allow five to nine position tension adjustment. This tensioning, tine diameter selection (sized 6mm to 8mm, or about 3/16" to 1/4"), three-point hitch height and gauge wheel setting combine to determine degree of soil penetration. Many makers allow individual tines to be raised up over crop rows while other tines are down for inter-row, postemergence cultivation. Well suited for cultivation of hilled crops such as potatoes, as tines can be adjusted to follow contour of field. There are many brands of weeders in Europe, where the tools are often used in small grains or to incorporate cover-crop seed. Frame clearance of 14" to 18" varies with tine length.

▶**Model for comparison:** 10' wide, or maker's smallest model
  Rec. PTO HP: 30   **Speed:** 4 to 8 mph   **List price:** $1,725 to $2,400

Width range (all makers/all models): 50" to 45'
  Larger models, 30' to 45', overall average $6,000 ($3,800 avg. U. S. sources, $7,400 avg. import)

Sources: 45, 56, 63, 65   **Farmers:** Chambers, deWilde, Haines, Reeder

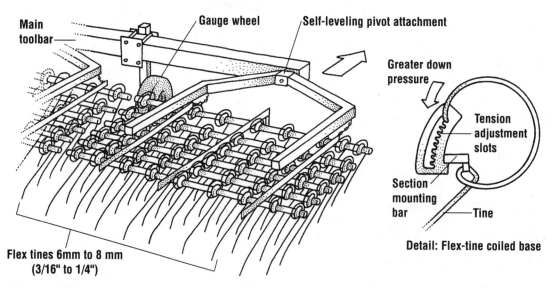

Main toolbar

Gauge wheel

Self-leveling pivot attachment

Greater down pressure

Tension adjustment slots

Section mounting bar

Tine

Detail: Flex-tine coiled base

Flex tines 6mm to 8 mm
(3/16" to 1/4")

Spike-Tooth Harrow

Crop, weed ranges similar to flex-tine weeder.

Overview: Pointed metal spikes stir soil to a depth of 1" to 1.5". For weeding, works much like a rotary hoe or flex-tine harrow (See "Harrows and hoes to the rescue," below.) Used widely for seedbed preparation.

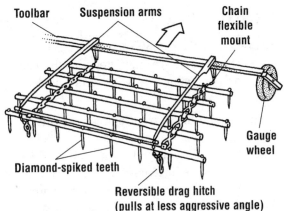

Design features: The high-carbon steel spikes (0.5" or 0.62" square, about 8" long) are set to run corner-forward as a diamond, and are bolted into "bars" of round pipe or square tubes. Five to nine bars in sequence pull about 10 teeth per running foot through the soil. Some units are reversible: one direction sets teeth nearly vertical for cultivating and deeper penetration, the other direction lays the teeth almost flat for a leveling action. Other units have a handle for adjusting the angle from 10 to 85 degrees.

▶ **Model for comparison:** 33' trailer type, flexing bar brackets
  Rec. PTO HP: 80 **Speed:** 5 to 10 mph **List price:** $4,260

Width range (all makers/all models): 4' to 76'

Sources: 36 (butterfly tine only), 53, 69, 78 **Farmers:** Erisman, Spray

---

HOES AND HARROWS TO THE RESCUE

Flex-tine weeders, spike-tooth harrows and rotary hoes can be set so that they perform shallow tillage weeding about the same as each other in non-crusted soils. But in heavily crusted soil, flex-tines may not penetrate at all and the harrows can dislodge then push soil chunks with weeds intact, damaging shallow-rooted crops.

In North Dakota, research with 20 crops showed the rotary hoe and a light spike-tooth had about the same impact on crops. Use was preemergence at crop-specific times then again at about two weeks after planting.

Both tools work preemergence in small grains until shoots (coleoptiles) reach the tillage zone depth of 0.5" to 1". They can be used postemergence after grains show their first true leaf through the 3-leaf stage. Later use will inflict yield-reducing stress on the crop. Postemergent use is not recommended for amaranth, canola, crambe, mustard and oats. Stand reduction occurs in buckwheat, flax, lentils and proso millet. Stand reduction is possible in safflower.

In general, a one-pass mechanical treatment followed by weed scouting and a species-specific, reduced-rate herbicide can provide suitable weed management at the same or lower cost as herbicides alone, according to agronomist Greg Enders of NDSU. For a 1997 chart listing mechanical weed control recommendations for 21 crops, write "Harrow List," NDSU/Carrington Research Extension Center, Box 219, Carrington ND 58421, fax (701) 652-2055.

Cultivators

Innovations in the past 30 years have made cultivators more farmer-friendly, crop sensitive and soil-conserving compared with earlier models. Consider

• **Three-point hitch, front or rear mounts.** If you remember cumbersome mid-tractor "belly" mount corn cultivators, today's models are a lot less hassle. Rear three-point hitches are standard. Quick-hitches make connecting and dropping off cultivators as easy as backing up, making contact, and locking on. Front-mount three-point hitches give clean visibility and quicker steering response.

• **Soil-conserving designs.** Flexing linkages, residue-cutting coulters, wide undercutting sweeps, greater clearance between components, narrow-profile shanks, and tall box crop shields have moved cultivation into high-residue, no-till systems. These components retain 50 to 90 percent of residue and minimize soil disruption in conservation tillage fields.

• **Precision and control.** Stronger toolbars and attachments that are more rigidly secured serve to reduce the "wobble factor," allowing operators to run tools within 3 inches of crops at high speed, a feat that demands tight conformity front to back. Tool gang members—mounting frames set at right angles to the main toolbar—can hold a set of tools that work between rows. Most are attached to the toolbars by parallel linkage—assemblies of pins, hinges and springs that consistently keep each sweep moving independently at its desired depth in uneven terrain. A range of guidance systems can provide constant tool alignment without a backward glance. They are described here after row-crop tools.

• **Adjustment.** A generation of farmers with skinned knuckles prompted the "wrenchless adjustment" cultivators, cranked screw-jack depth controls, single wrench systems, spring-pin adjustments and re-positioning of adjusting nuts in more accessible locations.

Crops, soils, weed species and tillage all influence the tooling of a cultivator and what it needs to do to manage weeds. This book presents four general cultivator types, categorized by their capacity to handle crop residue. Groups are titled "**low residue**," for conventional and reduced tillage that leaves up to 20 percent residue; "**moderate residue**" for up to 30 percent residue; "**high residue**" for up to 60 percent residue with minimum tillage of 120-160 bu/A corn; and "**maximum residue**" for 90 percent residue or more with no tillage of highest-yielding corn. Categories are further defined in each entry.

Cultivating loose, residue-free soils is the forte of **multi-sweep vibrating S-tine units**. These tines shake weed roots free from clinging soil. In firmer soils that resist sweep movement or in higher residue levels that plug close-set shanks, **rigid single shank** cultivators pull sharp sweeps that slice weeds just beneath the soil surface. Sweep profile, design style and wing angle determine whether soil is lifted unbroken, turned over, or moved into the row. **Rolling cultivators** are highly adjustable, aggressive, soil-stirring tools that can handle moderate residue and effectively work angled beds or flat fields.

TIPS: Run coulters 0.5" to 1" below point of sweep to effectively cut residue. Use disk hillers (where residue allows) to cut weeds and push them away from the row, or (when crops are established) to throw soil back onto the row to smother small weeds.

Low-Residue Cultivator

Intended for conventionally tilled, light to moderate soils with small stones and up to 20% tilled residue.

CROP height range estimate

| 0" | 2" | 4" | 6" | 8" | 10" | 12" | 18" | 24" | 30" | 36" |

WEED height range (annuals) estimate

■ suitable ▨ less suitable □ unsuitable

Match tillage timing, depth and location to crop root growth. Weed control varies with soil conditions and weed density.

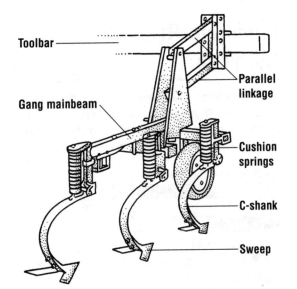

Toolbar — Parallel linkage — Gang mainbeam — Cushion springs — C-shank — Sweep

Overview: Uproots or buries weeds between rows in a growing crop; because the shanks are usually closely spaced (less than 6" apart), residue flow is restricted. May be adjustable for row width, sweep depth, sweep pitch and toolbar height. Constructed for minimal soil movement, light draft and minimal surface residue. Operate 1" to 2" deep for best weed kill and for highest moisture retention. Cultivating more deeply after applying a preemergent herbicide will bring untreated soil to the surface.

Design Features: Three to seven shanks per row are usually mounted on cross pieces attached to structural gangs and work between crop rows. A **parallel linkage** connects gangs to a main toolbar. This linkage allows vertical flex over higher surfaces that allows gangs to follow soil contours while they stay rigid side-to-side. Units used on bedded (raised row area) crops have two or three smaller parallel, rigid toolbars.

Low-residue, ground-engaging tools include shovels, points, knives and smaller sweeps up to 7" wide. Leading shank styles are **"Danish" S-tines** that vibrate vigorously to shatter and aerate soil, knock soil from weed roots, and leave weeds exposed on the soil surface; **straight vertical** (rigid mount) shanks with spring-trip feet which maintain an exact position until an obstruction pushes the sweep over center; and **C-curved, spring-cushioned** shanks made of thin, flat spring steel (pictured), which vibrate slightly and flex around obstructions or compacted spots of soil. S-tine shanks in these units are up to 18" tall with 24" of toolbar clearance.

▶ **Model for comparison:** 15', rigid frame for 6 rows on 30" centers (6R30)
Includes toolbar, shanks (any type), wide sweeps, one gauge wheel per gang, toolbar-stabilizing coulters, two rolling crop shields.
Rec. PTO HP: 50 to 90   **Speed:** 3 to 8 mph   **List price:** $2,800 to $11,940 ($5,586 avg., high/low deleted)

Width range (all makers/all models): 5' to 41'

Sources: 3, 15, 16, 20, 26, 47, 52, 55, 59, 63, 76, 78, 81, 95, 96, 102, 103, 105

Farmers: Erisman, Fernholz, Hattaway, Kenagy, McKaskle, Spray

---

Moderate-Residue Cultivator

Units intended for conservation tillage conditions (tilled residue with 30 percent coverage) or an untilled corn crop yielding up to 120 bushels/acre in loose to moderate soils with occasional stones up to 10 pounds.

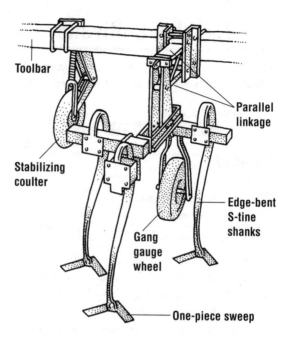

Toolbar

Parallel linkage

Stabilizing coulter

Gang gauge wheel

Edge-bent S-tine shanks

One-piece sweep

CROP height range estimate

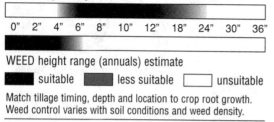

| 0" | 2" | 4" | 6" | 8" | 10" | 12" | 18" | 24" | 30" | 36" |

WEED height range (annuals) estimate

▮ suitable   ▮ less suitable   ☐ unsuitable

Match tillage timing, depth and location to crop root growth. Weed control varies with soil conditions and weed density.

Overview: These cultivators are a popular step up from a conventional cultivator for their ability to handle moderate weed pressure and moderate residue for less cost than a high-residue tool. S-tine tools have three to five shanks per row middle and generally weigh less than single-shank units. Choose sweep shape for your desired weed impact (i.e., bury, slice or uproot) and degree of soil/residue mixing. (See "Cultivator sweep options," page 24.) Operating depth is about 1".

Design Features: Compared with *low-residue* S-tine cultivators, these units usually have higher toolbar clearance (24" to 32") and longer front-to-back clearance (40" to 52"), allowing better flow between shanks, and between shanks and coulters, and overall stronger construction. Most have parallel linkage. Close-coupled, single-shank units are highly maneuverable and reduce power needed to lift them up. A residue-cutting coulter and residue-pinning gauge wheel design (see illustration, page 19) increases residue capacity.

▶ **Model for comparison:** 15' rigid frame for 6 rows on 30" centers (6R30)
   Includes parallel linkage; S-tine shanks; sweeps; two toolbar-mounted stabilizing coulters; gauge wheels for each gang.
   Rec. PTO HP: 70 to 120   **Speed:** 5 to 8 mph   **List price:** $2,815 to $12,225 ($4,588 avg., high/low deleted. Range reflects wide variation in structural strength and mass.)

Width range (all makers/all models): 5' to 44'

Sources: 3, 16, 26, 47, 52, 54, 59, 68, 76, 78, 91, 96

TIP: Sizing a cultivator and selecting its tooling are choices influenced by hydraulic lift-assist (page 26), tractor size and hydraulic-system capacity, front-weighting, tractor tire ballast and prevailing soil and residue conditions. Cultivators are usually the same width—or half the width—as the planter.

High-Residue Cultivator

Intended for no-till or ridge-till fields, tilled fields with up to 60 percent residue or untilled residue equivalent to a corn crop of up to 160 bushels/acre, moderate soils, stones up to 10 pounds.

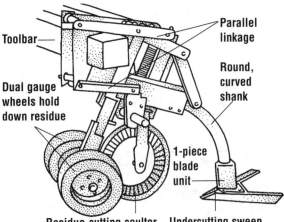

Toolbar

Parallel linkage

Dual gauge wheels hold down residue

Round, curved shank

1-piece blade unit

Residue-cutting coulter   Undercutting sweep

CROP height range estimate

| 0" | 2" | 4" | 6" | 8" | 10" | 12" | 18" | 24" | 30" | 36" |

WEED height range (annuals) estimate

■ suitable   ▨ less suitable   □ unsuitable

Match tillage timing, depth and location to crop root growth. Weed control varies with soil conditions and weed density.

Overview: Single-sweep cultivators were created in the '70s to work in substantial amounts of crop residue. Compared with S-tine units with multiple-shanks per gang, these tools can move more soil (including building ridges at last cultivation), work in tighter soils, and cope with more severe obstructions. Wide, flat sweeps of several designs undercut weeds and leave residue on the surface. Adjusting for more aggressive cultivation (tilting the sweep point downward) can push the sweep deep enough to disrupt incorporated herbicide layers in row middles, often releasing a new flush of weeds.

Design Features: Box-beam type main toolbars, fabricated steel-plate gang members and heavy-duty curved or straight shanks are common. Virtually all have parallel linkage, stabilizing coulters and residue-cutting coulters. Ground clearance ranges from 19" to 32", so match with your anticipated field conditions.

Front-to-back clearance varies greatly in this class. "Close-coupled" units set a single sweep immediately behind a residue-cutting coulter. This lightens the strain on hydraulics but sacrifices some residue-handling capacity. Longer gang frames facilitate residue movement, but these units usually require more hydraulic power to lift because sweeps are mounted farther behind the tractor's center of gravity. Optional **disk hillers** may work with close-coupled units in lighter residue conditions but won't have the clearance to handle higher amounts. They can be set to cut weeds and soil away from the row or to throw soil from between the rows back into the row. Operating depth is 1" to 2".

▶ **Model for comparison:** 15', rigid frame model for 6 rows on 30" centers (6R30)
   Includes toolbar; C-shank, box-beam or curved standards; wide one-piece sweeps; residue-cutting coulters; gauge wheels/gang; disk hillers.
   Rec. PTO HP: 75 to 120   **Speed:** 4 to 8 mph   **List price:** $4,800 to $11,110 ($7,959 avg., high/low deleted)

Width range (all makers/all models): 5' to 40'

Sources: 3, 7, 15, 20, 26, 46, 47, 54, 55, 59, 76, 90, 96

Farmers: Artho, Bennett, Berning, Cavin, Chambers, Erisman, Thacker

Maximum-Residue Cultivator

Intended for no-till or ridge-till fields, untilled residue equivalent to a corn crop of more than 160 bushels/acre, in moderate to heavy soils with occasional 500-pound rocks.

CROP height range estimate

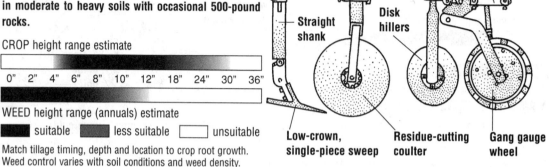

| 0" | 2" | 4" | 6" | 8" | 10" | 12" | 18" | 24" | 30" | 36" |

WEED height range (annuals) estimate

■ suitable   ▨ less suitable   □ unsuitable

Match tillage timing, depth and location to crop root growth. Weed control varies with soil conditions and weed density.

Labels: Box-beam gang mainbeam; Parallel linkage; Toolbar; Straight shank; Disk hillers; Low-crown, single-piece sweep; Residue-cutting coulter; Gang gauge wheel

Overview: These heavyweight units are built with the industry's top strength, soil-penetrating ability, and fore-to-aft as well as vertical clearance. Some can handle the residue of 250-bushel-per-acre corn, and others can subsoil between the rows. Weight may exceed 2 tons, so match the unit carefully with your tractor's hydraulic capacity, tire ballast and auxiliary weights.

Design Features: Massive 7"x 7" toolbars; sweeps up to 28" wide; wider and stronger parallel linkage (pivoting connections between the sweep gangs and the cultivator toolbar, flexing so that each gang can follow the surface contour but remain rigid side-to-side); and gauge wheels to control depth. Shanks are usually curved chisel-plow type standards or rigid vertical shanks, with some of the latter braced with welded steel plates. Adjustments include sweep angle to control penetration, disk-hiller spacing and angle (to direct soil flow), and coulter depth.

An auto-reset (trip-and-return spring) mechanism on some models allows a shank to extend backward over an obstruction when it exceeds the trip pressure. This option protects the tool while it maintains a uniform depth setting more consistently than a spring-cushioning shank.

▶ **Model for comparison:** 15', rigid frame for 6 rows on 30" centers (6R30)
   Includes toolbar; high-clearance shanks equipped with auto-reset springs; three-piece sweeps; and disk hillers, gauge wheels and residue-cutting coulters on each gang.
   Rec. PTO HP: 90 to 120   **Speed:** 5 to 8 mph   **List price:** $6,890 to $12,342 ($9,210 avg., high/low deleted)

Width range (all makers/all models): 8' to 44'

Sources: 2, 3, 7, 20, 26, 43, 51, 54, 59, 76, 90, 91, 96, 100, 102

Farmers: Bennett, Erisman, Kenagy, Hattaway, Thompson

TIP: To increase a tractor's ability to handle a heavier cultivator, try lift-assist wheels (page 26). To handle more compacted soil conditions, increase front-weighting or tractor tire ballast, as manufacturer specifications allow.

Rolling Cultivator

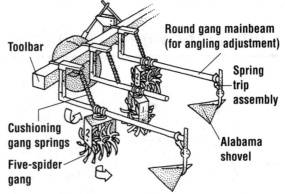

Toolbar · **Round gang mainbeam** (for angling adjustment) · **Spring trip assembly** · **Cushioning gang springs** · **Five-spider gang** · **Alabama shovel**

Intended for low-residue (spider gangs) or moderate residue (notched disk gangs) conditions.

Overview: A rolling cultivator tills with gangs of three to five spiders—wheels of strong, curved, cutting teeth radiating from a center hub—or notched disks. Disks are more aggressive than spider gangs and are more effective in residue. Gangs adjust three ways on round standards: to throw soil away from or toward the row; to move back or forward to align with other tools; and to change pitch to conform to the sides of raised beds. Can be used to build ridges. Heavy residue or larger rocks reduce the tool's effectiveness.

Design Features: The sharpened, angled ends aggressively slice through soil, uprooting and cutting weeds and leaving a fine surface soil mulch in loose soils. Split-row gangs position two spider wheels on each side of the row. They can operate very close to rows of crops up to 10" tall. Slicer tines run very close to a stationary bar to cut viny weeds.

▶ **Model for comparison:** 15' rigid toolbar for six rows on 30" centers (6R30)
   Rec. PTO HP: 70 to 90   **Rec. speed:** 5 to 10 mph   **List price:** $5,500

Width range (all makers/all models): 8' to 30'

Sources: 21, 48   **Farmers:** Bennett, Chambers, Foster, Gemme, Hattaway, Haines, Harlow, Muller

Horizontal Disk Cultivator

Parallel linkage · **Toolbar** · **Cushion spring** · **Disk sweep blades (rotate)** · **Vertical spindles (rotate)**

0"	2"	4"	6"	8"	10"	12"	18"	24"	30"	36"

WEED height range (annuals) estimate
▇ suitable   ▨ less suitable   ☐ unsuitable

Match tillage timing, depth and location to crop root growth.
Weed control varies with soil conditions and weed density.

Overview: In no-till or ridge-till fields where row middle soil is tight with roots, undercutting sweeps can cause slabbing of soil, leading to moisture loss and weed survival. Horizontal disks work in these conditions to uproot weeds, lift up the undercut soil then shatter it to knock soil from weed roots. Also work in loose or sandy soils. Moderate residue capacity.

Design Features: Self-sharpening disk blades (9" to 13") and round spindle covers spin freely to shed residue; 12" clearance fore-to-aft. Front two disks cut 1" deep close to the row and are canted slightly downward toward the row middle. The rear disk—usually set lower, at about 2"—cleans the middle and overlaps the front disks by 2" to 4".

▶ **Model for comparison:** 15' rigid toolbar for six rows on 30" centers (6R30)
   Rec. PTO HP: 60 to 70   **Field Speed:** 4 to 8 mph   **List price:** $9,600

Width range (all makers/all models): 10' to 36'   **Source:** 46

Cultivator Sweeps, Knives and Wings

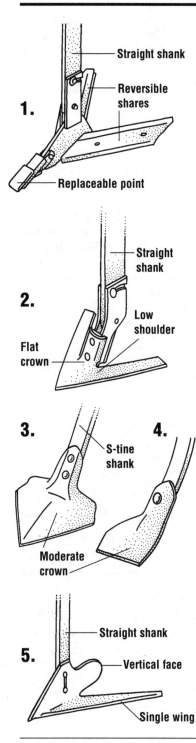

1. Straight shank / Reversible shares / Replaceable point

2. Straight shank / Low shoulder / Flat crown

3. S-tine shank / Moderate crown

4.

5. Straight shank / Vertical face / Single wing

1. Point-and-share (three-piece) sweeps (14" to 27" wide, for straight shanks) use a pair of replaceable, two-edged shares that usually lay flat to slice weeds. Replaceable point fractures soil, increasing penetration.
See: Erisman, Kenagy, Thompson

2. One-Piece, No-Till Sweeps (6" to 28" wide, for straight shanks) have a flat-crown, low wing (shoulder) angle. These sweeps leave row middles flat; slice through tall weeds and uproot shallow ones.
See: Bennett, Erisman, Hattaway, Kenagy, Thompson, Thacker

3. Pointed Row-Crop Sweep (4" to 7" wide, for S-tines). Better penetration than wider sweeps, more coverage than narrower shovels. Low-profile sweeps give similar soil mixing and weed impact as one-piece sweeps; moderate profile (higher center zone) causes greater mixing.
See: McKaskle

4. Duckfoot sweep (2" to 7" wide, for S-tines) provides good penetration of hard soil, significant soil mixing and weed uprooting (not slicing).
See: Chambers, Foster

5. Vegetable (Beet or Delta) Knife (8" to 30" wide, for straight shanks). For close cultivation in clean-tillage fields. A long, flat vertical face runs parallel to the row to protect the crop while a thin, flat sweep extends into the row middle. Mounted on straight or offset (dog-leg) standards.
See: deWilde, Foster, Haines, Kenagy, McKaskle, Muller, Thacker

6. Ridging Wings (on no-till sweeps) divert soil into row area to bury weeds and create an elevated ridge of soil for next year's planting at the same row position as the current year. Often width-adjustable and hinged to swing upward on the standard into a storage position during non-use. Usually used at last cultivation.
See: Thompson

6.

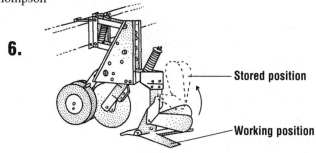

Stored position / Working position

Cultivator Shields

1.

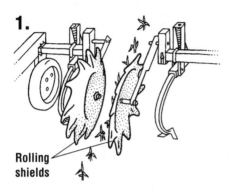

Rolling shields

2.

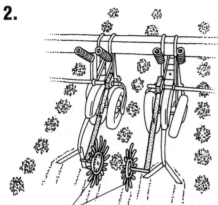

Rotary wheel shields

3.

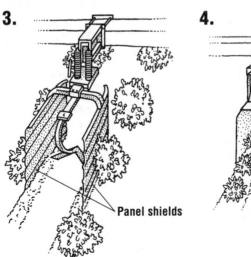

Panel shields

4.

Tall tent shields

1. Rolling Shield

Round disks made of heavy-gauge sheet metal, plastic or of actual notched disk-harrow blades rotate vertically on a hub next to the crop. Mounted as a pair over the row or split on the cultivator gang between the rows. They are often notched or pegged along the edge to assure positive rotation to help them roll over residue. Use of some over-the-row mounts may be limited by crop height.
See: Hattaway, Spray

2. Rotary (Hoe) Wheel Shield

Spinning wheel on walking arm protects crop from flowing soil and residue. The wheels aggressively uproot small weeds next to row or in the row—depending on setting—without penetrating deeply enough to damage crop roots.
Source: 105

3. Panel Shield

Flat metal pieces 10" to 24" tall and 2' to 3' long can handle high-volume residue and soil flow. Various mounts either over the row or between rows, usually on parallel linkage to follow soil contour.
Source: Widely available **See:** Thompson

4. Tent Shield

Smaller sizes of these U- or V-shaped cover-the-row shields allow soil to flow up and over their tops. Taller models are basically heavy-duty panel shields joined at the top for strength and durability. Up to 3' long, 3" to 8" wide and 6" to 30" tall.
Source: Widely available
See: Thompson, Muller, Spray

Cultivator Components

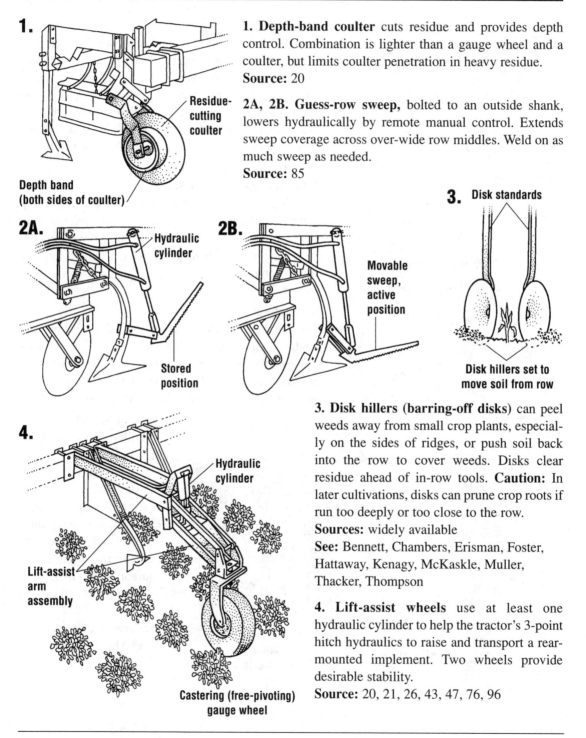

1. Residue-cutting coulter

Depth band
(both sides of coulter)

2A. Hydraulic cylinder

Stored position

2B. Movable sweep, active position

3. Disk standards

Disk hillers set to move soil from row

4. Hydraulic cylinder

Lift-assist arm assembly

Castering (free-pivoting) gauge wheel

1. Depth-band coulter cuts residue and provides depth control. Combination is lighter than a gauge wheel and a coulter, but limits coulter penetration in heavy residue.
Source: 20

2A, 2B. Guess-row sweep, bolted to an outside shank, lowers hydraulically by remote manual control. Extends sweep coverage across over-wide row middles. Weld on as much sweep as needed.
Source: 85

3. Disk hillers (barring-off disks) can peel weeds away from small crop plants, especially on the sides of ridges, or push soil back into the row to cover weeds. Disks clear residue ahead of in-row tools. **Caution:** In later cultivations, disks can prune crop roots if run too deeply or too close to the row.
Sources: widely available
See: Bennett, Chambers, Erisman, Foster, Hattaway, Kenagy, McKaskle, Muller, Thacker, Thompson

4. Lift-assist wheels use at least one hydraulic cylinder to help the tractor's 3-point hitch hydraulics to raise and transport a rear-mounted implement. Two wheels provide desirable stability.
Source: 20, 21, 26, 43, 47, 76, 96

Hot Tips For Flame Weeding

If flaming is a new technology for you, learn all you can about its principles, hardware and management from farmers, manufacturer reps, local LP-gas technicians and hands-on demonstrations. Competence, confidence and regular maintenance checks are the basis for safe operation of LP-gas tools. Keep these suggestions in mind as you select your equipment and set up your field for flame weeding.

1. Choose hardware to fit your weeding needs. The rate of fuel consumption per acre is influenced by burner capacity (measured in BTUs per hour), air temperature, gas pressure, plant surface moisture and the size of weeds being targeted. Compared with dry seedling weeds, wetter weeds and bigger weeds are harder to kill. You can deliver more heat with a slower tractor speed (giving a longer flame exposure), more gas pressure (giving a more intense exposure), or a combination of both.

Flame-weeding specialists or burner manufacturers can help you select the burner type, regulator setting, tank size and overall set-up that fits your combination of weeds, crops, soil condition and field size. Always use "motor fuel" rated tanks (approved by the U.S. Department of Transportation) for tractor mounting.

Fuel use can vary from 3 to 14 gallons per acre, depending on the intensity of the flaming and how extensive the coverage (a narrow band along the rows, or broadcast coverage of the entire swath).

2. Add cultivators with caution. Burners positioned behind cultivator shanks may enhance the benefit of cultivation, but probably will decrease the kill rate that flaming alone would have achieved. The moving soil and dust tend to deflect heat from the weed leaves. Running the burners out in front of the cultivator sweeps can also reduce the flaming kill rate. Weeds wilted by the flame that would dry out on the surface may recover if they are buried and protected by loose, moist soil.

3. Prevent flame deflection. Soil contour next to the row must be smooth and on a fairly consistent angle to assure optimum weed kill and minimum plant damage. Protruding clods or uneven terrain may shield small weeds or deflect flame into the plant canopy.

4. Lightness adds flexibility. Some farmers mount flamer parts on old cultivator toolbars—an inexpensive option, but often much heavier than needed. Mounting the burners and the tank on a simple pipe frame with runners makes a lighter unit that can be used in wetter soil conditions or with a smaller tractor.

In-Field Tips

Once you've got the hardware, focus on hitting weeds early. Flaming can set back larger weeds, but zapping weeds as tiny seedlings or before they have three or four leaves is best. Killing small weeds, you will have more predictable success at field speeds and fuel use competitive with mechanical or herbicide passes. For guidelines, flaming experts say

• **Don't burn weeds.** If weeds are toasted, you're wasting fuel. Energy-efficient flaming will have little immediate visible effect but will cause weeds to droop and wilt within a few hours. You want to travel as fast as possible, using the lowest gas pressure (hence the least amount of fuel) that kills weeds.

• **Timing is everything.** In stale-seedbed flaming, growers cultivate the growing area to stimulate surface weed-seed germination, with weed flushes controlled one or more times to deplete weedy competitors. When weed pressure and planting schedules allow, delay the final broadcast flaming until just before transplanting vegetable crops or planting quick-germinating, direct-seeded crops. This gives the crop the least weed competition during its most vulnerable stage.

Early postemergence flaming works, too, for crops that send up early leaves before their growing point emerges. Even if the young leaves are singed, these crops will bounce back as long as the growing point survives. (See de Wilde, p. 71.) Once the growing point emerges, allow substantial growth before flaming stalks.

• **Run when it's hot and dry.** Band flaming for between-the-row weeds—just like cultivating or rotary hoeing—is most effective at killing weeds in the heat of day with a gentle drying wind, not the cool dewy morning when it's more comfortable for the driver or in the evening when visible flames make it more dramatic. The more you want a drink of lemonade, the more you need to be out flaming weeds.

• **Adjust for accuracy.** For flaming between rows of emerged crops, leave time for careful adjustment of burner height and angle (both vertical and horizontal), fuel pressure, tractor speed and regulator setting. Take time to carefully examine young crops for flame damage to stems buds or leaves. Quick test: firmly squeeze a plant leaf between thumb and forefinger. Let go. If you see a finger print where you squeezed, the heat has burst cell walls and the leaf will wither.

• **End the fireworks.** Yellowish flecks or bands within the flame indicate foreign material within the combustion zone or blockage at the burner. Carefully clean out nozzles each year to remove carbon and rust that can flake off the inside of the steel pipe that leads to the burners. A bluish center flame is desirable.

• **Protect crops with water shield.** Spraying a thin layer of water over the plants with flat-fan nozzles helps protect them from the flame's heat. The sensitive plant parts of cotton, string beans and other crops can be protected with a wall of mist.

• **Maximize the benefits of beneficials.** Researchers notice that ladybird beetles survive higher temperatures than do tarnished plant bugs, a serious cotton pest. The beneficial beetle preys on the pests in both their larval and adult stages. Further, the tarnished plant bug appears at about the same time that cotton plants can first tolerate flaming.

PUBLICATIONS

ATTRA - Appropriate Technology Transfer for Rural America, P. O. Box 3657, Fayetteville, Ark. 72702. (501) 442-9824, (800) 346-9140, FAX (501) 442-9842. email askattra@ncatfyv.uark.edu Provides information packets of material on flaming and many other farm topics.

Farm With Flame, Joseph L. Smilie, et al, Louisiana State University (1965), 16 pp.

Flame Cultivation Equipment and Techniques, Production Research Report No. 86, USDA/ARS in cooperation with Mississippi Agricultural Experiment Station (1965), 16 pp.

INDIVIDUALS

Richard Parish, Hammond Research Station— Louisiana State University, 21549 Old Covington Highway, Hammond LA 70403, (504) 543-4125, fax (504) 543-4124.

Dale D. Moyer Suffolk County Ag Extension agent, Cornell Cooperative Extension— Suffolk County Office, 246 Griffing Ave., Riverhead NY 11901-3086, (516) 727-7850, fax (516) 727-7130. email dmoyer@cce.cornell.edu Moyer demonstrates toolbar flamers for insect and stale seedbed weed control. An eight-minute video describes a flamer set up for Colorado potato beetle control on potatoes. Cost of the video is $15, $20 outside the U.S.

Dr. Charles E. Snipes, Plant Physiology Weed Control, Delta Branch Station—Mississippi State University, Stoneville MS 38776, (601) 686-9311.

Row-Crop Flamer

(standard U.S. LP-gas, liquid feed)

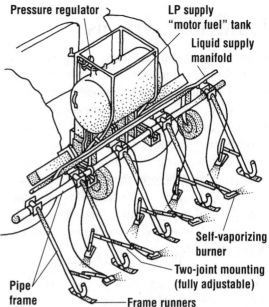

CROP height range estimate

0"	2"	4"	6"	8"	10"	12"	18"	24"	30"	36"

WEED height range (annuals) estimate

■ suitable   ▦ less suitable   ☐ unsuitable

Match tillage timing, depth and location to crop root growth.
Weed control varies with soil conditions and weed density.

*Postemergent heights for crops with a heat-resistant stalk, such as corn or cotton, that allow cross-flaming in row. Flame contacts stalks. Optimum stages for in-row flaming corn are up to 2", 8" to 12", then 18" to 24."

Diagram labels: Pressure regulator · LP supply "motor fuel" tank · Liquid supply manifold · Self-vaporizing burner · Two-joint mounting (fully adjustable) · Frame runners · Pipe frame

Overview: Flames from LP-gas burners kill plants by rupturing cell walls, not burning plant tissue. Flaming is most effective on broadleaf weeds as small seedlings. It is less effective against grasses, and least effective on sedges and weeds that branch at ground level. **Broadcast flaming** can cover an entire bed or toolbar width prior to crop emergence. **Directed flaming** targets a specific zone between crop rows or in-row beneath plants after they develop a heat-resistant stem.

Design Features: LP gas flows as a liquid that vaporizes in high-BTU burners. This arrangement avoids the "freeze-up" potential of vapor-withdrawal systems, caused when gas is burned faster than it can vaporize directly from the main tank. Burners can be mounted on steel-frame skids or on cultivator toolbars. Tanks *must* be motor-fuel rated. Do not use stationary propane tanks.

▶ **Model for comparison:** 15' with gauge wheels
Rec. PTO HP: 70   **Speed:** 3 to 5 mph   **List price:** $2,200 to $5,000†

† Lower price for add-on kits to adapt cultivators; $2,200 for kits assembled with used cultivator frame and used tank; $5,000 for entire new unit.

Width range (all makers/all models): 4' to 30'

Operating cost: 3 to 14 gallons per acre per application, depending on tractor speed and gas pressure, which are in turn influenced by crop, field and wind conditions. Code-complying tanks range in price from $275 (used 110 gal.) to $550 (new 250 gal.). Tank rental $25 to $60 per season, where available from LP-gas or crop-protection material companies. Two or three applications per season are normal; more may be necessary, depending on weed pressure.

Sources: 33, 61, 98

Farmers: de Wilde, Foster, Harlow, McKaskle, Thacker   **Also:** See hand flamers on p. 63.

Note: Fueling renewed interest in flaming are herbicide-resistant weeds and regulations on worker pesticide safety and water pollution. Flamers pose no threat of carryover or runoff but do require a thorough understanding of LP gas safety.

Guidance Systems

Even with well-adjusted tools doing excellent work, driving a tractor to cultivate hundreds of acres is a tedious job that demands uncommon powers of concentration, alertness and quick response to occasional obstructions. Guidance systems use mechanical, hydraulic and electronic methods to detect cultivator movement in relation to the crop row, then move the tractor, the hitch or the tool to restore the desired alignment. Adoption of guidance systems is nearly routine on 12-row and larger equipment in the upper Midwest.

Benefits include relief of driver stress, closer cultivation to the row, great precision on sloping fields—especially on contour strips—and increased acreage covered due to faster speeds. (See "Precision guidance technology can pay its way, " page 110.)

Mechanical guidance systems use wheels or panels that follow soil contours. These tracking devices physically hold the cultivator to the location of an elevated soil berm (in beds or ridge-till rows) or furrow.

Electronic guidance controls take their cues from slender wands or dragged furrow weights suspended from the toolbar. The wands run along the soil surface near the base of crop plants, while furrow weights run in row middles. A shaft connects these wands or weights to a switch box on the toolbar. Sensors within the box detect shaft rotation when the cultivator moves away from its centered alignment, then signal the hydraulic system to make its compensating motion. Residue, protruding dirt clods or stiff weeds can compromise accurate crop sensing.

More sophisticated systems use micropro-

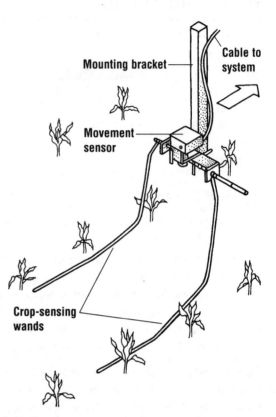

Guidance system sensors often use wire or plastic wands that run near the base of crop plants. The wands attach to a bracket that pivots whenever one of the wands moves closer to the row and is pushed back by crop contact. Micro-switches relay the sensor signals to a control unit, which activates the degree and duration of toolbar correction needed to realign the wands with the row. Weights attached by chains can follow furrows, and V-wheel sets can sense a ridge top, both attaching to the same sensor bracket.

cessing computers and on-board diagnostics. These allow the operator to vary the sensitivity and frequency of the system's response, and to monitor a digital or graphic readout of the tool's alignment.

TIP: Automatic guidance systems of any type increase wear on parallel linkage and other joints due to frequent re-centering movements.

Guidance Mirrors

Overview: Mounted to the tractor frame below and in front of the driver, this mirror provides a clear view of the crop row behind the tractor to show cultivator location and movement. Allows close monitoring while facing forward. Work best before corn is 12" tall and leaves begin to obscure view of row.

Design Features: Universal mounting with one or two bolts; closing door for protection during road travel; rugged housing.

List price: $100   **See:** Thompson
Source: Klinger Mfg., RR 1, Box 186A, New Ulm MN 56073

Housing   Mirror

Furrower/Wheel Guidance

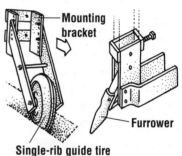

Mounting bracket

Overview: Furrow-following guidance systems perform well in fields that are fairly flat and relatively residue- and rock-free. At planting or final tillage pass, a furrowing ripper forms a distinct trench shaped to securely guide a sharp-edged steel wheel or thin, ribbed rubber tire attached to the cultivator toolbar. Positioning the guide wheel at the end of the toolbar, creating firm furrow sides and running the guide wheel deeply are steps to maximize control. Use with sway blocks up or removed so that hitch arms swing freely.

Furrower

Single-rib guide tire to follow groove

Design Features: Guide-shoes or custom sweeps create a V-shaped furrow; steel wheels or flared boots smooth and firm furrow walls; single-rib or highway tires—depending on design—ride in the furrow to guide the tool.

List price: $1,500 to $1,900 (Note: Includes two furrowers and two complete guide tire assemblies.)
Sources: 3, 14, 21, 81, 90
Note: Electro-hydraulic systems also can use furrows by dragging special weights as sensing units.

Ridge Mechanical Guidance

Pivot pin   Auxiliary toolbar

Overview: This rugged, all-mechanical system keeps planters or cultivators in line whenever there is sufficient ridge height to guide its dual, rubber tire V-wheels (pictured, straddling ridge top) or metal Bell wheels (pushing against ridge sides). The ridge-following wheels swivel at their anchor point. As the tool's orientation to the ridge changes, the wheels shift an adjoining coulter that in turn guides the implement. Low yoke axle of V-wheels limits use to crops of 6" tall or less.

Turnbuckle adjustment

Design Features: Adjustments extend the system's use over many conditions, but the consistency of the ridge shape is critical to its effectiveness.

Flat steering coulter   Tie rod adjustment   Rubber V-wheels

List price: Single set, $2,200 (6-row cultivator); double set, $4,295 (8 to 12 rows).   **Source:** 35

Hitch Steer Guidance

(electric sensing, hydraulic adjustment)

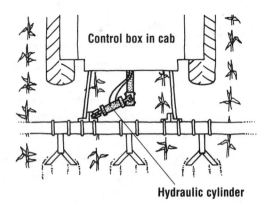

Control box in cab

Hydraulic cylinder

Overview: Using a simple electric switch, this system provides dependable service with readily available parts. It tracks tool position relative to the row with crop-sensing wands, then compensates for tractor drift by hydraulically adjusting the cultivator toolbar left or right. Stabilizing coulters may be used on the cultivator but are not required. Remove sway blocks so that hitch arms may move freely, permitting the cultivator to stay positioned on the row despite tractor deviation. System does not influence tool's operation, but crop plants have to be stiff enough to activate sensor.

Design Features: A sensing unit with mechanically triggered micro-switches monitors the crop or a furrow. It signals a solenoid-operated hydraulic valve when the cultivator moves off-center. The valve controls a double-acting, 8" hydraulic cylinder bolted to the tractor drawbar by a special channel-iron bracket. The other end is most often attached to the implement toolbar at a weld-on connection at one of the hitch plates. The low-pressure (500 psi) system works well up through 30-foot-wide cultivators on moderate (2 to 4 percent) slopes. The kit includes a cab-mounted control box with indicator lights, weighs less than 100 pounds, and works with or without a quick hitch.

List price: $1,750 (excludes cylinder and hoses, available for about $100).   **Source:** 2

Side-Shift Guidance

(electronic sensing/controls, hydraulic adjustment)

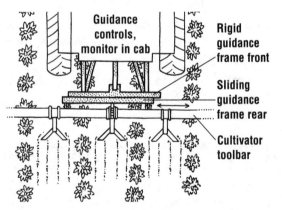

Guidance controls, monitor in cab

Rigid guidance frame front

Sliding guidance frame rear

Cultivator toolbar

Overview: A side-shift unit works best with straight rows and on cultivators with shorter fore-to-aft clearance. Suitable for conventionally tilled or no-till fields. It keeps the cultivator toolbar parallel to the tractor axle at all times. Insert sway blocks to hold hitch arms rigid. Stabilizing coulters not necessary with side-shifters. System does not influence tool's range of crop or height capacity.

Design Features: These units have two interlocking parts with a quick-hitch tool attachment: a front frame that mounts to the tractor's three-point hitch, and a rear plate to which the implement is attached. By blocking the tractor swaybars, the front frame remains stationary. A hydraulic arm pushes against it to move the rear plate left or right in response to the sensing device's signals through an electro-hydraulic steering control box. In-cab electronic monitors show movement and maximum adjustment. Dual rear tires or bias ply rear tires increase tractor stability, helping to transfer shifting force from tractor to cultivator when needed.

List price: $4,800   **Sources:** 20, 44, 58, 91

Tool-Pivoting Guidance

(electronic sensing/controls, hydraulic adjustment)

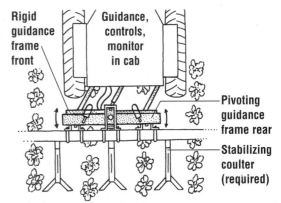

Overview: A pivoting guidance system requires stabilizing coulters and loose (unblocked) three-point hitch arms. It effectively compensates for the "tailout" effect with long tools when the implement end and tractor front move in opposite directions. This effect is aggravated with articulated tractors and when working on contours. With sufficient coulter anchoring, pivoting systems work well even in heavy soil and with implements that have substantial sideways draft resistance. Accuracy is best when sensors are mounted toward the center of the toolbar. System does not influence tool's range of crop or height capacity.

Design Features: Quick-hitch attachment. Common to both leading types of pivoting systems are two opposing hydraulic cylinders that work in concert. They simultaneously push and pull on the two lower implement attachment points, moving one side slightly ahead as the other side moves slightly back. Their movement slants (pivots) the toolbar just enough to point the sweeps in the desired direction to keep the cultivator properly situated. Rigid stabilizing coulters provide the rearward anchor that steers the implement in the desired direction.

List price: $4,500 to $4,900   **Sources:** 20, 26, 58, 76, 91, 92, 102   **See:** Thacker

Disk-Steer Guidance

(electronic sensing/controls, hydraulic adjustment)

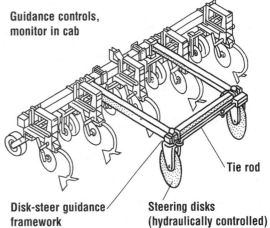

Overview: One of the earliest electronic-sensing guidance systems, steering disks are now used primarily in the most severe conditions or with 12-row or wider equipment. Sophisticated electronics provide self-diagnosis and automatic calibration, important features for wide tools when a control lapse could affect so many rows at once. System does not influence tool's range of crop or height capacity.

Design Features: The system uses two to six 27" disks mounted on a rigid box-beam frame that sets the disks several feet *behind* the toolbar, usually straddling two to eight rows per set. Sensing signals control hydraulic movement of the tie-rod that connects the disks, turning them as long and as sharply as needed for alignment. Allow draft arms to move freely. Pivot-type stabilizing coulters work best on the cultivator. Designed for closed-center hydraulics; adaptable to open-center systems.

List price: $7,100 for controls and two-disk set-up (guides 8-row unit)   **Source:** 76   **See:** Cavin

Ridge-till Planter

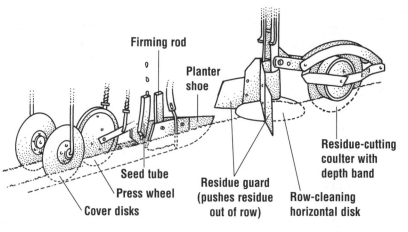

Firming rod
Planter shoe
Seed tube
Press wheel
Cover disks
Residue guard (pushes residue out of row)
Residue-cutting coulter with depth band
Row-cleaning horizontal disk

Ridge tillage uses permanent elevated rows 30" or more apart that keep traffic off the row area.

Cultivation is central to ridge tillage. Suitable cultivators can handle residue and work 4" to 6" deep. Disk hillers need to be height-adjustable to run higher than sweeps for early passes. At first cultivation (corn more than 3" tall, soybeans more than 2"), disk hillers skim weeds from sides of the ridge (moving soil into row middles) while wide sweeps run lower to undercut weeds in row middles.

Second cultivation controls later weeds just before crops form a shade canopy and also creates ridges for the next season. A narrower sweep prevents damage to developing crop roots. The disk hillers are set to move soil back into the row. The best (flat or gently rounded) ridges are formed by ridging wings, which are mounted on cultivator shanks. The wings push soil—flowing back from sweeps and disk hillers—into the row area, rebuilding the ridge. The soil moved into the row smothers weeds, preserves moisture in the root area and anchors stalks against lodging. Minimize soil hilling in soybeans that could interfere with harvest of low-hanging pods.

Ridge-tilled fields are left undisturbed—except for optional stalk chopping—until the next planting season. Residue tends to accumulate in the middles, but also protects the ridges over winter. Elevated stalks and ridge height helps trap snow—a benefit in dryland areas. In the spring, ridge tops dry and warm more quickly than unridged ground. Ridge tillage is especially suited to flat fields of slow-drying or heavy soils, in contoured rows on slopes up to 6 percent, or for furrow-irrigated fields.

Ridge-till planters are unique in their ability to be configured to significantly suppress weeds (see page 111). The planters do two things: 1. Skim a thin layer of weed seed-laden soil and residue from the old seedbed's row area; 2. Plant crop seeds by placing them into firmed, moist soil then covering them with loose, drier soil. Preventing weed seed-soil contact delays weed growth in the row area, giving the crop an advantage.

Design Features: Tooling may include a residue-cutting coulter with depth-gauge wheels or a depth-banded coulter (to cut residue and provide uniform cleaning depth); a wide sweep, horizontal disk or double vertical disks (to move soil from the row area and create a weed-free seedbed); trash guards or residue wings (to push disturbed soil and residue into row middles); a seed press wheel; and small cover disks and/or a harrow trailing to cover the seed row.

List price: Six rows on 30" centers
        Conversion kits: $225 to $900   Complete planters $15,200

Sources: Whole goods: 20; Conversions: 1, 25, 41, 43, 97 **See:** Thompson

Agronomic Row Crops: The Farmers

Thompson farm trials confirm efficiencies of covers, hoes, cultivators

Dick & Sharon Thompson
Boone, Iowa
- *300 acres* • *corn, soybeans, oats, hay, cover crops*
- *ridge-till for row crops* • *slightly rolling fields in central Iowa*

Weed management highlights
Strategies: early weeds managed to suppress late-germinating weeds... no preplant tillage... increased plant population... 36" rows... fine-tuned cover-crops

Tools: customized ridge-till planter... high-residue rotary hoe... high-residue cultivator... guidance mirror

Dick and Sharon Thompson and their son, Rex, didn't just write the book on sustainable weed control—they update it with improvements every year. A high-residue cultivator and high-residue rotary hoe are prominent among other sustainable tools and practices in the scientific on-farm testing they have conducted since 1985. (For their latest report, send $12 to Thompson On-Farm Report, 2035-190th Street, Boone IA 50036-7423.)

No part of their cropping system exists long without being scrutinized for improvement. They still use cover crops, but have long ago moved away from fall-broadcast mixtures of winter rye and hairy vetch. Vetch posed too many management problems come spring.

For cover crops ahead of soybeans, their experiments found the most weed-suppressing benefit from rye alone, drilled at 20 pounds per acre only on the ridge top—two rows, 6 inches apart, each 3 inches from the crop row. A ridge-till planter can remove spring growth of 8 to 12 inches. Taller rye can be knocked down with a stalk chopper. (See "Cover Crops," page 110.)

Corn's need for early nitrogen and moisture

means rye is not a good cover crop choice for corn planted on ridges, the Thompsons found. Rather, they overseed oats at 2 bushels per acre with a high-clearance tractor at leaf-yellowing of soybeans—usually in late August. Freezing weather kills the oats, but stalks remain on the surface to protect the soil from spring erosion.

When they plant corn into a flat field following hay, however, they spread rye through Gandy seed boxes during fall plowing of the hay field as they incorporate strawy manure. The greater weed-suppressive effect of rye is needed for this transition, and standard spring soil preparation allows a way to control the rye that is not available in their no-herbicide, ridge-till-only system. **Field cultivators** kill most rye at the 6- to 8-inch stage, with scratchers dragging behind to bring the residue to the surface. After waiting about a week for the disturbed weed seeds to germinate, a second field cultivation takes out almost all the rest of the rye. At final weed cultivation with his **maximum-residue, single-sweep cultivator,** Thompson attaches **ridging wings** just above sweeps to divert soil into the row to create the elevated ridges that will be used the next several seasons.

"Crop rotation is the key," says Dick Thompson, who tries to maximize soil-building and weed-fighting benefits from the farm's mixed enterprises. Components include hogs, beef cattle and livestock manure, with aerobic digestion of municipal biosolids. The five-year crop sequence is corn-soybeans-corn-oats-hay (legume/grass mix).

Weed populations take a beating from this varied sequence of soil environments, preventing annuals and perennials from strengthening their populations. Existing weed seeds sprout between rows or between plantings—the places and times when light tillage or mowing can control them. Multiple cuttings in hay years knocks back species that thrive in undisturbed soil. The winter cover crops of rye and oats are selected and managed to mesh precisely with the intended crops to follow.

For row crops, Thompson uses ridge tillage, a system that plants rows in the middle of raised soil areas—ridges—that dry out and warm up faster in spring. By planting into the same row area each year, the system controls implement traffic. Ridge-till also can cut labor and fuel costs compared with conventional tillage because there is no pre-plant tillage and less soil is disturbed.

Ridge-till's permanent rows and necessary ridge-restoring cultivation provide the bridge from broadcast spraying to herbicide banding for some farmers. The next reduction can be to lower material rates within the bands. For Thompson and others, ridge-till's weed seed movement into the row middles at planting and faster, closer cultivation have allowed him to virtually eliminate chemical weed controls in most years. In any tillage regime, straighter rows can translate into easier, more efficient mechanical weed control with a lower risk of crop damage.

Thompson advises all farmers to refine management through their own on-farm testing. He offers these cumulative findings for evaluation:

• **Manage early weeds to control later weeds.** Thompson claims this is the "best-kept secret in agriculture." He observes that the first weeds prevent more extensive germination of later-developing weeds. This may result from compounds released from roots or other factors such as shading and moisture competition. He regards early weeds as a natural cover crop. Despite their potential for good, early weeds need to be controlled in the row at planting with timely rotary hoeing or at first cultivation while they are small enough to be easily managed and before quick-maturing species go to seed.

Thompson's row-cleaning, ridge-till planter moves weed seeds and cover-crop residue into row middles as a mulch that protects soil and stifles weed development. (See "Ridge Till Planters Suppress In-Row Weeds," page 111.)

• **Select a planter that fluffs loose soil over firmly planted crop seed.** This leaves crops in a good environment for germination but puts weed seeds in a poor environment for getting started. Be aware that packer wheels working on the surface or trailing scratchers improve weed germination rates, he warns.

• **Plant crops thicker** for quicker in-row shading and to allow for some reduction in plant population from mechanical tillage. Twelve soybean seeds per foot and corn seed at 6-inch spacings work best, Dick Thompson finds.

• **Rotary hoe before and after crop emergence.** He keeps a close eye on planted corn, waiting for seeds to sprout before using his M&W Gear **high-residue rotary hoe**—but he faithfully hoes soybeans three days after planting, weather permitting. The different approaches result in the same end: he hoes both crops just before emergence thanks to the longer time corn usually waits in cooler soil.

> *"Managing weeds with crop rotation, ridge tillage and steel is $54 per acre more profitable for us than with broadcast herbicides and mulch tillage."*
> — Dick Thompson

"You have to get off the tractor to check the hoe's penetration, weed kill and crop response," says Thompson. He looks for crop seed disruption or seedling damage. "Then I know how fast to drive and how deep to go." These preemergence passes are shallow (about an inch) and fast. "Fifteen miles per hour is about as fast as I can hang on," he admits. Extreme weed pressure justifies an immediate second trip, which Thompson does by half-lapping the previous round.

He waits about a week before hoeing a second time. At this point, corn is at about the two leaf stage (the third leaf is just beginning to emerge from the whorl) and soybeans have true leaves. These early "broadcast" tillage passes are important to suppress weeds when they are easiest to kill, and especially to control in-row weeds.

His M&W Gear **high-residue rotary hoe** handles residue well. Thompson believes that hoes need at least 20 inches between front and rear shafts to handle heavy residue. Rotary hoeing returned an average of $16.20 per acre more than even *banded* herbicides did in a three-year weed-control comparison, Thompson reports.

• **Outfit your cultivator** for young crops—and have it ready to run! His standard practices at first cultivation include

   - **Disk hillers** with the leading edge angled into the row and cupped forward to make a cut as wide as possible that still moves soil away from the row. The hillers are set 5 inches apart—but even "tighter on the row that I watch," explains Thompson, to narrow his margin of error.

   - A **"Culti-Vision" rearview mirror.** This hooded, adjustable guidance aid is mounted on a bracket attached to the tractor frame just behind the front axle. It is aligned so the driver can see exactly where the hillers are running next to the crop. The mirror improves the driver's control enough to run about 3.5 mph at a stage when crop plants are too small to activate the **sensing wands** of an electronic guidance system. By also using a wide-angle, rear-view mirror inside the cab, Thompson can scan all four rows without turning around.

"Guys who use herbicides can afford to wait for four-inch corn that will activate guidance system wands. But those of us who are all-mechanical have to be out there earlier to stay ahead," he says. One species he particularly targets for early control is lambsquarter. Once the tap-rooted competitor is 6 inches tall, it becomes difficult to kill with a cultivator. Broadleaf weeds that have less of a tap root are easier to control when they are taller.

• Use of 26-inch **one-piece sweeps** in 36-inch row spacings. "I need to be able to increase the pitch to get some soil-turning action," Thompson finds. "The flat, narrow surface of **point-and-share sweeps** basically undercuts weeds. I want to be harder on my weeds than that."

• **Metal tent shields** with 18-inch rear extensions dragging in the soil. The shield fronts stay down if rows are clean—to keep out fresh soil with its newly exposed weed seeds—but are raised slightly to allow loose soil to flow in if enough small, in-row weeds are threatening. The rear extensions add extra stability and crop protection. At second cultivation, he replaces the tents with open-top, **flat panel shields** to avoid bending crops.

• **Stopping, dismounting and stooping low** to inspect crops and weeds. Where he plans a hay crop and doesn't need ridges the coming year, Thompson does a second cultivation with wide sweeps *before* crops are a foot tall. He changes the angle of the disk hillers to throw soil *toward* the crop row, and moves them farther away from the row to avoid throwing soil around the plants. In soybeans, this prevents damage to lower pods and keeps mounded soil from interfering with harvest. In corn it limits root pruning that can hurt yield. His tests show that ridging in fall after corn harvest and removal of stalks can increase weed numbers in the following year's soybeans.

In wet seasons when crops are much more than a foot tall before he can make a second pass, Thompson uses a 14-inch sweep without ridging wings to avoid cutting crop roots.

Where he wants to build a ridge, Thompson begins the second cultivation with 14-inch sweeps *after* crops are a foot high. At that point the plants can tolerate contact by flowing soil that smothers in-row weeds. He moves the disk hillers to the row middles and turns them to push soil into the row. A "butterfly" **ridging wing** mounted on the shank behind each sweep diverts soil from the middles to the row ridge, smothering in-row weeds. Two sets of open-top row shields ride several inches off the soil surface next to the row to protect crop stalks and leaves.

Because bigger plants block his view of the hillers via the Culti-Vision mirror, Thompson removes it and uses his pivot-type **automatic guidance system** as crops mature. The electronic-hydraulic unit guides the implement to keep it in alignment with the row. Guidance greatly eases driver stress and allows Thompson to travel about 6 mph.

Night cultivation and tilling has yet to show consistent benefits in USDA-supervised tests on Thompson's farm. In other trials, the practice has reduced post-tillage germination of small-seeded broadleaf weeds. As part of his on-farm research in '96 with researchers from the National Soil Tilth Laboratory in Ames, he used night-vision goggles for nocturnal ridge-till planting. The goal is to deprive light-activated weed seeds the illumination necessary to trigger germination.

Improved implements and mechanical techniques hold the best opportunities for making weed management more sustainable, says Thompson. "If you use herbicides and still don't control weeds, you're building herbicide resistance. If you do control your target weed, you get weed-species succession and end up with weeds that are harder to control." He can trace a troublesome weed progression from horseweed to foxtail to velvetleaf during his own farm's "chemical era."

In '95, the Thompsons and other farmers who successfully practice integrated weed control with negligible herbicides formally described their systems to gatherings of weed management professionals. From those sessions, Dick Thompson sees a new appreciation for the importance of "alternative" practices.

"Weed scientists are finally taking field ecology seriously, talking about 'managing' weeds rather than 'controlling' them, and saying herbicides should be the last resort. I think they're on the right track." ■

More weed control with fewer passes

Peter Kenagy
Albany, Oregon
• *300 acres* • *wheat, grass seed, sweet corn, snap beans* • *diverse cover crops*

Weed management highlights

Strategies: strip tillage into herbicide- and winter-killed covers... banded herbicides... field borders in mowed sod crops... prevention of off-site introduction of weed seeds

Tools: Maximum-residue cultivator... rotary hoe... front-mount conventional cultivator.. rotary tiller

Cover crops on Peter Kenagy's farm in Oregon's Willamette Valley may be wavy, green and 6 feet tall, or bushy, scarlet and knee high. All serve to improve soil quality, prevent erosion and help him manage weeds in row crops, with the help of strip-till planting and a maximum-residue cultivator.

He manages the species, germination date and method of killing of each cover crop so that it contributes optimum benefits at crucial points throughout his cash-crop season. Species that regrow each spring after the region's mild winters increase their biomass contribution and outcompete early weeds.

Warm-season Sudangrass, by contrast, follows his earliest commercial snap bean crop. The tall, thin stalks smother summer weeds with their profuse vegetation that dies with the first frost. He has to plant Sudangrass for cover-crop use *after* mid-July to avoid seed set but *before* August 10 to achieve sufficient growth before frost.

Kenagy's succession of at least four sweet corn plantings starts in the dead Sudangrass, where he applies Roundup to control bothersome winter annuals. Roundup is a non-selective, non-residual systemic herbicide. He plans a 10- to 30-day window before planting. During that time, weed biomass and an apparent post Roundup flush of soil microbial activity die down, clearing the way for better corn seedling development. His spring barley germination suffered in '96

within areas where he had applied Roundup to suppress ryegrass the same day that he planted.

Kenagy developed pieces of his sustainable low-spray, strip-till planting system for sweet corn in '95. Testing cover-crop species and ways to kill them, he successfully

• No-till seeded the corn in April into volunteer wheat killed by herbicides 2 weeks earlier growing in unmowed wheat stubble.

• Strip-tilled the corn into a rape/oats mix that had been grazed by sheep the previous fall then killed with herbicides in March when it was 18 to 24 inches tall. He tries to terminate the cover crop before it grows too much biomass to accommodate the strip tillage.

• Herbicide-killed annual ryegrass at the end of April with Roundup.

• Flail-mowed crimson clover at 18 inches tall in early June.

• Let sheep graze triticale (a wheat-rye cross) in April and early May, then let leaves regrow enough to make herbicide effective in late May. In '96, a dry spell just before planting prompted him to also flail mow the stemmy stubble to create a moisture-retaining mulch.

All told, Kenagy planted 100 acres of sweet corn in '96 by rotary tilling 6-inch strips into cover crops of the rape/oats mixture, crimson clover and winter-killed Sudangrass. Weather problems caused the clover to mature past its "easy to handle" time. He had to tediously flail-mow it at about 2 mph after it had bloomed and become quite fibrous, disk it twice with his 12-foot offset disk, then power-harrow it to break up clumps of biomass. His corn did well, but he admitted the delayed start increased labor, fuel and machine use to uncomfortable levels.

The **rotary-tilling cultivator** he converted for strip-till planting works just well enough that he and other growers in his area who are interested in pursuing the practice agree that they need to find a more versatile and sophisticated strip-till planting tool.

The Yetter Residue-Manager wheels on his John Deere 7000 planter eliminate surface irregularities that could create uneven planting depth. Well-aerated and elevated about 2 inches higher than the undisturbed row middles, the tilled strip warms faster to speed crop development, Kenagy reports. He sees 85 to 90 percent germination in the tilled strips, compared with a 50 percent rate when he no-tills the same non-vigorous varieties of sweet corn that he grows on contract for processing.

Kenagy applies a 10-inch band of a grass and broadleaf herbicide mix over the rows at planting to suppress early weeds. He evaluates each field's weed pressure to put on just enough herbicide to hold back in-row competitors until he cultivates. He delays the first pass of his **maximum-residue cultivator** until weeds eventually pop through the cover crop residue between the rows. While the specialty corn usually demands a weed-control pass at about its 5-inch stage under conventional tillage, he doesn't cultivate the strip-tilled corn until it is about 10 to 14 inches tall. He says not disturbing the soil or residue in the row middles slows weed seed germination.

"I used to cultivate two or more passes in sweet corn because weeds were a problem earlier," he explains. He gets by now with only one—sometimes two—trips with his Buffalo 6600.

For Kenagy, the 20-inch, **point-and-share sweeps** on the heavy-duty tool take out redroot pigweed and lambsquarters of about any size, but he has trouble with purslane plants re-rooting. He sets disk hillers 3.5 to 4 inches from the row, throwing soil to the row middles. He responds to variable conditions at second pass by just moving the hillers out slightly, possibly turning them around to lightly cover in-row weeds, or removing them if weed pressure is negligible.

He adjusts the cultivator to minimize ridging by the sweeps. Even a slight crest interferes with the ground-level swather needed to harvest the following ryegrass seed crop. The moderate corn residue is not a problem at ryegrass planting or harvest, he reports.

Kenagy has full view of his low-tech, front-mounted cultivator from the seat of his Farmall M. He uses the narrow-front "tricycle" tractor rig for precision cultivating his string beans in clean-tillage situations. They usually follow a wheat or grass-seed crop that is disked (unless heavy residue requires plowing). He then uses a spike-tooth harrow or a Lely Roterra, a PTO-powered harrow with horizontally spinning vertical club tines.

His traditional multiple-toolbar cultivator has horizontal gang mounting bars suspended from its main 10-foot toolbar. The gang bars give him infinite tool spacing adjustment. Closest to the row, he runs 8-inch **disk hillers** that move little soil at his low-speed (3 to 4 mph) operation but push out weeds within 2.5 inches of the row. He sets 14-inch, L shaped **vegetable knives** within 4 inches of the row, with the sharpened blade edges trailing out and backward toward the row middles.

"The knife's vertical shank curves inward at the base, putting the inside blade edge closer to the plant than the top of the shank," Kenagy explains. "This is gentle on the crop, slices out small weeds and doesn't throw around any dirt."

Two 10-inch **goosefoot sweeps** on straight, rigid shanks take out weeds between the 30-inch rows, while rear-mounted **S-tines** loosen the tractor wheel tracks.

Kenagy needs a flat inter-row area for efficient harvest of low-hanging snap beans. To level the soil, he pulls mounted gangs of old cast-iron roller wheels between the rows at last cultivation. Because he harvests and replants covers within a month of the treatment, weeds don't have time to set seed or reduce bean yield.

He runs the front-mounted unit without shields. But with his single-sweep, **maximum-residue cultivator**—operated at 5 mph—he needs to protect plants with open-top, **flat panel shields.**

Kenagy counts his often-rebuilt, 10-foot flail mower among his weed management tools. He no-till plants a mixture of perennial forage ryegrass, white clover and a tall forage-type fescue to smother weeds that could invade on windborne seed from uncropped areas.

The complementary legume/grass smother-cover combination assures Kenagy that at least one heavy-rooted species will protect soil and suppress weeds. The ryegrass establishes quickly, clover often flourishes where grasses can't, and the fescue comes on strong in the second year to become a traffic-tolerant survivor.

Kenagy is zealous about removing weed seeds from any equipment he brings onto his farm. "I clean everything—sweet-corn toppers to seed-cleaning equipment to squash loaders."

Kenagy is a patient, methodical innovator who considers weed management a natural part of raising crops—not as a way to conquer an enemy. Recall his approach to sweet corn. On some farms, corn means herbicides, fertilizer and bare soil. For Kenagy, the interplay of customized cover crops, strip tillage, spray banding and minimal cultivation make his sweet corn plantings a rotation phase that actually *lowers* weed pressure. ∎

No-chemical control regime integrates timing, tools, covers

Carmen Fernholz
Madison, Minnesota

• *300 acres* • *four-year crop rotation* • *conservation tillage (30 percent residue)* • *feed/cash crops: corn, soybeans, spring wheat, oats, barley* • *cover crops of red clover, annual alfalfa, berseem clover*

Weed management highlights

Strategies: delayed planting into warm soil... crop rotation... high-tilth soil with increasing organic matter... mechanical controls

Tools: low-residue C-shank cultivator (front and rear mounts)... standard rotary hoe... field cultivator... chisel plow

Canada thistles have kept Carmen Fernholz from trying to pioneer drilled no-till, no-herbicide soybeans. His sustainable system already earns him honors in production efficiency, but he wants to build on that successful foundation through even more cost-effective weed control.

In '96, scientists working on his farm with an experimental *Pseudomonas* bacterium had "tremendous success" infecting—and controlling—the prickly pests and other weeds. Fernholz's goal is to combine this natural weed disease with especially competitive, weed beating soybean varieties. That's the kind of persistent innovation that allows him to manage potentially serious competition from wild sunflowers, foxtail and cocklebur while reducing tillage passes. His approach is to coordinate a host of compatible practices, each of which helps to lower weed pressure.

Fernholz combines tilth-building soil management, keen soil temperature observation and precisely timed tillage during the early season to check weeds. His cultivation quest is to disrupt weeds close to the plants early in the crop cycle, with a minimum of soil disruption. He knows excess tillage burns soil organic matter and increases erosion risk.

Fernholz has shown that his basic system makes money (and saves soil) through his entries in the MAX program—a maximum economic yield analysis established by *Successful Farming* magazine. In '92 his 51 bushel per acre soybean entry following a hairy vetch plowdown with 18 percent residue earned a net profit of $99.63 per acre, as calculated by the MAX formula. That ranked him in the top 25 percent of bean entries from 16 states. The entry's weed control consisted only of three cultivations. His soil loss was estimated at 1.8 tons per acre—substantially below his county's average soil allowable figure of 5 tons per acre.

In '93, cool weather reduced yield to 43 bushels per acre and MAX profit to $33.16 per acre, using a standard $5.35 per bushel sale price. But his certified-organic beans sold for $9.75 per bushel, giving him an actual profit of $222 per acre on the no-herbicide, soil loosening crop.

His top four weed-management points are

• **Cover crops to improve soil structure.** Red clover, NITRO annual alfalfa and berseem clover are his favorite covers because of their ability to loosen up soil. Fernholz wants a crumbly, coarsely granular structure to create the optimum environment for vigorous development of crop roots. It also maximizes the weed-killing effect of his implements, allowing them to uproot weed seedlings and not create clods or slabs.

He seeds these soil-builders at 12 to 15 pounds per acre ("lots of seed to assure a strong, competitive stand") in his small grains, which serve as nurse crops. Strong stands keep opportunistic fall grasses from invading.

He applies manure immediately after grain harvest, lets the legume grow through late fall, then chisel plows the field about 7 inches deep. The result is a rough surface that traps snow and enough residue to prevent erosion.

When the soil is warm, he uses a **field cultivator** (9-inch sweeps with 3 inches of overlap) to eliminate surviving legume plants and spring weeds. He makes two passes about 4 inches deep—one at 45 degrees to the row, the second with the row. "Moving from six inch sweeps with hardly any double coverage up to the nine-inch sweeps made a 'night-and-day difference' in the tool's weed-killing ability," he reports. Adding to their effectiveness is their "full-width" engineering which causes the sweeps to maintain their full cutting width as they wear down.

The passes take care of the first round of redroot pigweed and foxtail, which germinate at about 50°F—the same temperature as corn. He seeds corn into warmed, weed-free soil where the crop has the best chance to out-compete the next round of weeds.

• **Planting tied to soil temperature.** To kill more early weeds with tillage and to give his crops faster germination, Fernholz waits to till and plant until his soil remains at 50°F or higher for several days. Because daily temperatures in the planting zone fluctuate considerably as the soil gradually warms in spring, he waits until he finds consistent readings with his soil thermometer located 5 inches deep.

Waiting on warm soil means Fernholz starts planting corn about three weeks later than his "early-bird" neighbors. But he sees quicker emergence, often within 8 to 10 days—and often ahead of corn around him planted earlier into colder soil. His robust corn seedlings move more quickly through their development, lessening the period they are most vulnerable to competing weeds before producing a weed-shading canopy.

• **Rotary hoe pass five days after planting**—"unless it's too wet." Fernholz faithfully makes this pass whether or not he sees any weeds breaking through the surface. "You don't know how important the pass was until it's too late," says Fernholz. You can use a non-sprayed skip as your "weedy test" control plot. He uses a 30', flex-wing, standard John Deere **rotary hoe.**

He runs it at just 5 to 6 mph—about half as fast as the speediest operators—and also breaks the normal practice by raising the gauge wheels to allow the teeth to penetrate way down to about 4 inches. "I have virtually no crop damage because anything with a good root stays put at the slower speed. But the deep aeration really bothers the thin grass roots and gives me excellent control."

He's found the best conditions for knocking out weeds come on dry days when air temperature is at least 75°F and there's a 10 to 12 mph wind, regardless of the implement used. In moister or cooler conditions, hoeing can still benefit the crop by setting back weed growth.

• **Simple, appropriate tooling.** Fernholz uses a low-residue, conventional John Deere cultivator retrofitted with low-profile, 6-inch sweeps on flexing, flat-stock, curved C shanks. (Chisel-plow type shanks—used on maximum-residue cultivators—are the same shape but are much thicker steel and rigid.) The sweeps glide through the top 2 to 3 inches of his loose soil with hardly a ripple in the flowing action. They run flatter than the former sweeps (that were mounted on vertical standards) thanks to the forward-sloping angle of the C-shank's attachment point. By staying consistently shallow, the flatter sweeps don't gouge down to scour up lumps of soil that threaten young corn plants as the old ones did.

Crop damage, loss of alignment with the row and even toolbar damage was a problem with the more pitched shovels on the unit's old straight shanks. "Yes, the cushion springs were supposed to protect against rocks, but after a few seasons outside, the springs become too stiff to flex," Fernholz found out. The lively action of the C-shank gives a consistent soil flow with much less adjustment during use. This is because "It's virtually immune to disturbances from rocks," Fernholz says. Consequently, the new hardware means he can set the sweeps closer to the row, experience less crop loss, drive faster, and worry less as he goes through the field.

He usually cultivates twice per field—three times if wet conditions allow weeds to resprout. Target depth is about 1.5 inches. He stays shallow to preserve moisture and stimulate as few weed seeds as possible.

Seven sweeps per row give weeds no place to hide. Fernholz runs four sweeps per row on a frame-mounted, front toolbar positioned just behind the front axle. He doubles coverage with three sweeps per row on a rear-mount toolbar to obliterate wheel tracks and further disrupt surface weeds.

Even with excellent soil tilth that boosts water infiltration, Fernholz knows that each tillage pass burns up humus—the most soil-enriching form of organic matter—and leaves his fields more vulnerable for a time to water-caused erosion. He's focusing his management research on corn, the one year out of four he will still have relatively exposed soil in a row crop during early summer rains once he breaks the barrier to organically certifiable, solid seeded beans. ■

Covers and cultivation check no-till weeds

Rich Bennett
Napoleon, Ohio
- *600 acres* • *no-till rowed beans* • *corn, soybeans, spring wheat*
- *minimum-till corn in 30-inch rows* • *cover crops: cereal rye, hairy vetch*

Weed management highlights

Strategies: Crop rotation... cover crops... herbicide kill or incorporation of covers... timely cultivation

Tools: High-residue cultivator... disk harrow

Rich Bennett has mastered an alternative low-input system that features planting soybeans into herbicide-killed grain rye or hairy vetch, cultivating crops twice, and cutting input costs for his 250 acres each of corn and soybeans.

His alternative practices help him avoid primary dependence on herbicides to combat the weed species shift to foxtail and panicum that become more challenging after several years into no-till. He pays close attention to timing tool use and quickly makes tool adjustments to accommodate changes in crop size and weed conditions.

Bennett began reducing fall tillage and using cover crops in 1989 to control wind erosion and minimize soil disturbance. A two-year on-farm research grant helped him hone the use of fall-planted grain rye to control weeds in soybeans. (The funds came from the USDA's Sustainable Agriculture Research and Education program.) He figures he saves at least $15 per acre compared with standard no-till soybean systems.

Besides providing a moisture-conserving mulch and weed-shading canopy, rye residue kept on the surface holds down weeds through allelopathy—a natural suppressive effect on one plant by compounds produced by another. This natural weed control allows him to skip rotary hoeing and postemergent herbicide in soybean fields. But rye can hurt bean yields if it mats heavily or takes up too much soil moisture in a dry spring.

Bennett plants rye in late October so that it emerges but shows little growth before winter dormancy. He broadcasts rye at 2 bushels per acre after disking cornstalks just once. "I got away from choosing corn having bamboo-type stalks that needed two diskings to break down," says Bennett.

He plants soybeans on 30-inch rows into the standing rye as soon as conditions allow in May, at 70 pounds per acre to ensure an adequate stand. His White no-till planter provides uniform placement and depth for soybean seeds and works well with different seed sizes. "I leave the no-till coulters off and just use the disk opener. The coulters would stir up soil and stimulate foxtail and other weeds," he notes.

Bennett reduces the amount of rye he knocks down with field-equipment by spraying it on the same pass that he plants beans. The tender rye is about 2.5 feet tall and providing plenty of shade. Roundup—applied at only 1.5 pints per acre—kills the rye, while 1 quart of Lasso controls nightshade. Adding 1.7 pounds of ammonium sulfate and 13 ounces of surfactant per acre increases herbicide absorption, giving Bennett good control with half the label rate for Roundup.

If you're not using herbicide burndowns, be sure to chop the rye by late boot stage and before it heads, cautions Illinois organic farmer Jack Erisman (page 46). He often overwinters cattle in rye fields that precede soybeans. But he prefers to wait until the soil temperature is at least 60 degrees before planting beans. That's too late for no-tilling soybeans into standing rye. "If rye retillers and gets away from you, you'd be better off baling it or harvesting it for seed," Erisman notes.

When his beans are 8 to 10 inches tall, Bennett sets the front edges of the **disk hillers** on his Buffalo Model 6300 **maximum-residue cultivator** about 3.5 inches on either side of the row. The disks peel back grasses and other weeds. He cultivates at about 4.5 to 5 mph, with the single sweep nearly flat, running 2.5 to 3 inches deep.

"I put just enough pitch on the **one-piece sweep** so it throws dirt nicely into the row. Even in cold, wet springs, rye puts on good growth and gives plenty of mulch. The **rolling cultivator** I used to use couldn't make it through all the biomass," he says.

Bennett clears up the row middles two weeks later with a second cultivation. For this, he removes the metal, **open-top panel shields** necessary for protecting small crops. He also takes off the disk hillers or reverses positions and moves them away from the row to avoid throwing too much soil into the bean row. Other settings and speed are the same as for first cultivation. With a typical harvest of 45 bushels of soybeans per acre—5 to 10 more than county average—Bennett is pleased with how well his rye/soybean system works.

Right after harvesting hairy vetch about the first week of August, Bennett thoroughly disk harrows the stubble in his recently combined wheat fields. He used to broadcast 25 to 30 pounds of hairy vetch seed per acre using two staggered, overlapping passes with a 40-foot-wide spreader.

In '96 he drilled hairy vetch seed to improve seed-to-soil contact and to eliminate his usual post-broadcast tillage with a disk and a rolling cultipacker. "I must have been getting the seed tilled in too deeply. In '95 demo plots, 23 pounds drilled seed gave a better stand than broadcasting 30 pounds per acre," observes Bennett. Using his conventional drill won't eliminate any preplant disking, though, as he has never gotten a good vetch stand unless he incorporates the wheat stubble.

With the help of Ben Stinner, an Ohio State University researcher who directs many farmer-oriented efforts in sustainable farming, Bennett is working to increase the efficiency and fertility value of hairy vetch in his no-till corn. Using vetch can lower fertilizer and herbicide bills but also can help give some weeds a faster growth rate. Here again, Bennett's single-sweep, no-till cultivator keeps row-middle weeds in check.

He had used 2,4-D to kill his vetch cover crop, but he's turned to disking to get a quicker release of nitrogen and to ensure an adequate seedbed for corn. He disks knee-high vetch in late April or early May. After the first pass with his tandem, smooth-bladed disk, he checks the field in several spots to flake back the top 2 inches of soils. "If I see a lot of viney material in there, I redisk. I don't think I need to cover the vetch completely with soil," he says. "But I do need to prevent vetch regrowth and ensure good seed-to-soil contact for the corn."

In '96, the quicker vetch breakdown boosted N available just before final cultivation to 100 pounds per acre. This was 50 percent higher than the usual nitrogen contribution from vetch killed by herbicide but left on the surface and tested at the same time. Consequently, Bennett reduced the amount of supplemental N he applied to 60 pounds per acre—50 pounds per acre less than he usually applies at layby. His yields on conventional corn and low-input (vetch-enhanced) corn average about the same—160 bushels per acre.

The increased fertility also increased potential weed pressure, so Bennett applied a 10-inch herbicide band of Frontier at the full rate equivalent of 23 ounces per acre. When he has more stalks on the surface from unincorporated herbicide-killed vetch, he applies Lasso at a band rate equivalent to two quarts per acre, with atrazine at a rate equal to 1.5 pounds per acre. Banding has cut his preemergent herbicide costs by two-thirds in his 30-inch rows.

Just before the corn's third-leaf stage—i.e., when the third leaf just begins to emerge from the whorl—he broadcasts 1.5 pints of 2,4-D per acre for bindweed control.

Bennett waits until about the fourth-leaf stage before he cultivates. Grasses are his biggest challenge due to the abundant nitrogen from cover crops and hog manure, and he wants to clean up lambsquarters or foxtail survivors. "Where I don't till annually or deeply, the weeds don't start quickly and my first cultivation knocks out virtually all of them," he says.

He usually cultivates corn at the same settings and speed used for soybeans. He does a final cultivation by the time corn is knee-high to 2 feet tall.

Bennett knows the ability and limits of his weed-control implements. He strives to combine other management practices to control weed pressure because "hitting the weeds within my cultivation window is crucial." ∎

A sustainable transition takes the right metal

Jack Erisman
Pana, Illinois
• *1,800 acres (all certified organic)* • *80-cow, cow/calf beef herd*
• *legumes: sweet clover, red clover, alfalfa* • *row crops: corn, edible soybeans* • *orchardgrass/clover/alfalfa pasture mix* • *mulch tillage with disking* • *cover crops: rye, buckwheat, hairy vetch* • *small grains: oats, wheat, canola, rye, triticale*

Weed management highlights
Strategies: Minimum tillage... cover crops... seven-year, flexible crop rotation... mechanical cultivation

Tools: Flexible-chain harrow... high-residue rotary hoe... three cultivators (low-residue, high-residue, maximum residue)... heavy and light tandem disks

Jack Erisman uses both conventional and unconventional practices to protect his soil resources and production potential. Terraces he built long ago now seem less important to him than thick-rooted cover crops for erosion control. He has a wide inventory of tillage and cultivation tools not because he likes to use them, but so he can use each one as little as possible to its best advantage.

Building his soil's biological quality and its loose, crumbly structure are his primary goals and serve as the foundation for successful integrated systems of non-chemical weed control and crop production. His on-farm research is geared to finding the tillage-cutting building blocks of organic, no-till systems for soybeans and other cash crops.

Erisman has been practicing conservation tillage for more than 25 years, having used a modified ridge-till system in the late '60s and early '70s. He began testing organic management methods in '88 and quit using synthetic fertilizers and herbicides in '90.

He's kept his farming herbicide-free since then and completely organic since '93. He credits a flexible rotation for part of his success. For a typical seven-year rotation he plants an overwintering rye cover crop followed by soybeans; a fall-planted small grain; a legume/grass mix "frost-seeded" into the grain in late winter; several years of hay or pasture; corn; another rye cover-soybeans sequence; cereal grain frost-seeded with a legume/grass mix; finishing with a fallow year when the forage mix growth is clipped but left to replenish soil organic matter.

The seventh year's "crop" is enrichment and regeneration of soil biological life. Erisman calculates that the soil benefits which improve and protect succeeding crops easily offset his opportunity cost plus clipping and $20 per acre in taxes. A late seeding of buckwheat for grain in the seventh summer and then a fall seeding of rye to restart the rotation combine to provide a needed break in the legume cycle that prevents a buildup of soil disease organisms.

To fit fields and control weeds for his broad crop mix, Erisman has an array of cultivation equipment.

• He likes how his M&W Gear **high-residue rotary hoe**'s single wheel-per-arm design provides enough weight and downward pressure to aggressively expose weed seedlings, for example. "A double toolbar hoe can seem smoother, but you'd need more springs and bearings in crusty settings," he observes. Soil crusting isn't the norm in Erisman's silty clay loam fields.

He usually hoes at least once and up to three times if warranted, at speeds from 5 to 10 mph, depending on soil conditions. Often, he'll double back so that wheels work different areas. "You could cover more ground faster with a dou-ble-toolbar hoe and save fuel. But I think I get more aggressive action by lapping back. To concentrate the best weed control where it's needed most for a modest cost, Erisman replaces hoe wheels over the row more often than those that run between the rows, where his cultivator will clean up the survivors.

• His heavy-duty, 8-row Buffalo 6300 **maximum-residue cultivator** handles field residue without any trouble and adjusts easily for different conditions. On first cultivation of soybeans, Erisman usually turns **disk hillers** to throw soil into row middles and spaces them 7 inches apart, then reverses them for the next cultivation. He travels 7 to 8 mph with the Buffalo for each cultivation, using big 24-inch **one-piece sweeps** on 36-inch rows, typically operating 1.5 to 2 inches deep or deeper, depending on the mulch.

"One disadvantage of the Buffalo is its weight. But that also stabilizes it well," says Erisman. He went to a heavier tractor with improved hydraulics and rarely counterbalances the front with more than a thousand pounds.

• To avoid soil compaction in mellow fields, he uses a lighter, compact Orthman Super Sweep **high-residue cultivator** for second or third cultivations when he can. The wide point-and-share sweeps clean out row middles nicely in late season if wet or dry conditions have encouraged weeds. "The different share sizes let me adjust clearances pretty easily and I run it without front disks or shields."

• In low-residue situations—typically fields where cattle have grazed—Erisman uses an old International 153 **low-residue cultivator** with multiple 8- to 10-inch sweeps and straight shanks. He runs it at about 4 mph at a depth of 1 to 1.5 inches about 7 inches from the row for first cultivation of soybeans, using panel shields to protect crops. He occasionally uses it for second cultivation, when he just takes off shields and speeds up to 6 to 7 mph. He adjusts the sweep pitch from flat up to 2 inches, depending on how much soil he wants to throw and how worn the sweeps are.

Erisman waits for corn or bean plants to be at least 4 inches tall before he cultivates, but he also evaluates plant stability. Spindly plants that have developed in cool, wet weather need to be taller to withstand even slight soil movement, he says.

A **coil-tine harrow** would be even better than the 32-foot Fuerst flexible-chain harrow Erisman relies on, but they're hard to find in his area, he says. Depending on soil conditions and planting depth, he typically harrows beans the third day after planting, at anywhere from 5 to 8 mph and a depth of a quarter- to a half-inch. The harrow works best in his loose soils where its fixed points cause rapid surface turbulence that disrupts weeds. The rotary hoe, by contrast, works best in his fields with tighter or crusted soils where its arms shatter soil and fling out weeds.

Wants Fewer Passes

Erisman's shift to organic crop production systems increases overall tillage due to crop rotation and mechanical cultivation. Rather than an adverse impact on the soil, he's seen changes for the better. "Green manure crops cushion the tillage impact," he says. "Our soil structure has improved—it's more granular and friable than it was."

Hand digging and visual observations by researchers from the USDA National Soil Tilth Lab showed significant differences in soil tilth structure on his farm compared with neighboring farms. Erisman credits the distinction partly to his use of deep-penetrating legumes, such as alfalfa and sweetclovers, and minimal use of deep tillage.

Erisman has fields in different stages of organic transition and many crop sequences to juggle. Critical management situations include

"I'm trying to cut my field passes as another way to improve soil structure and soil life. Good management systems with year-round crop cover buffer what we do when we use tillage or cropping practices that compromise the soil environment."
— Jack Erisman

Rye to soybeans. His main rye-killing tool is a John Deere 32-foot offset disk. In wet years, he starts with a flail mower to stop growth and buy time until field conditions permit disking. Final preplant weed control and soil conditioning comes from his 36-foot **field cultivator.** Rye requires careful management to coax out all its benefits. "Rye residue can keep ground cold, and its allelopathic (weed suppressing) effects are gone after about three weeks," says Erisman.

Rye needs to be killed before it puts on explosive growth just before it heads out. Rampant growth can dry out the soil in moisture-deficient years, or present too much biomass to easily incorporate or plant through, depending on a farm's equipment. Mowing *after flowering* stage is a no-herbicide, no-till control option.

In '96 he used a John Deere no-till planter to establish a third of his edible soybeans into easily cultivated 36-inch rows—his standard method. He planted the balance of his beans as solid-seeded fields with a 37-foot Wil-Rich air seeder. The unit blows seeds through plastic tubes that scatter them under its 7-inch cultivator sweeps, which also eliminate small weeds during planting. Because air-seeders work whenever conditions permit field cultivating, he doesn't have to wait for soil to be as dry as a planter requires. This option reduces tillage passes in fields with low weed pressure.

In solid-seeded fields, cultivation is not

possible, so Erisman depends entirely on relatively low weed pressure going into the season, harrowing or rotary hoeing after planting and the quick establishment of a crop canopy to keep weeds to a tolerable level.

The air seeder's improved metering system allowed accurate seeding rate control, which Erisman adjusted between fields from a low of 210,000 seeds per acre up to 280,000 seeds per acre. Fewer weeds were visible in the heaviest seeding. 1996 was the first year he planted all his soybean fields with saved seed of varieties prized by the world's organic buyers.

Pasture to corn. To move from hay or pasture into corn he also uses his disk in early spring if conditions are ideal. If rain intervenes, he will disk or field cultivate successive flushes of weeds until he plants. If a penetrometer (a slender pointed rod used to test soil resistance) detects "disk pan" compaction, Erisman uses a standard subsoiler in the hay field just before the soil freezes. He runs the hyperbolic points shallow, at about 6 inches, just below the disk layer to increase the mellowing effect of winter freezing and thawing.

Soybeans to grain. The air seeder allows him to dispense with disking after soybeans, and to blow in the grain seed by pulling the cultivators through undisturbed soybean residue.

His long-term goal is to reduce tillage trips wherever he can and to minimize the downside risks of trips that he continues to make. "For a serious broadleaf weed problem in a flood prone area, maybe with cockleburs, moldboarding might be the most effective single operation you can do," Erisman explains. "But don't repeat it often. And do it after soil temperature has reached its summer plateau—when earthworms have burrowed down deep—and drier conditions prevent soil compaction."

He considers judicious disking to be a necessary evil that ensures timely field preparation for planting. "My preference is not to do a lot of disking. But when you have two to three tons of cover crop residue per acre, it can be your best option." His 32-foot John Deere 630 tandem disk harrow covers a lot of ground quickly. He installed 22-inch, notched blades on 7.25-inch spacings to increase residue incorporation.

Market Rewards Organic Transition

By planting late, he has had excellent weed control but has to deal with a yield penalty that puts him 5 to 10 bushels of soybeans per acre behind the county average. "If you can learn to manage weeds and grasses, 50-bushel organic yields are quite feasible. I've had 40 bushel beans with solid seeding even with half the field covered with foxtail."

Corn yield is more of a problem because he has yet to find food-grade varieties that are bred to thrive in his moderate-fertility setting. He currently plants white corn, which seems to be somewhat less dependent on optimum fertility.

"I'm midstream in my organic transition and still learning. But I can compete very favorably with organic market premiums to cover the extra management that healthy soil requires," says Erisman. "I'm ready now to try earlier planting dates, make management compromises and take my yield chances with early-emerging weeds, knowing now that I can almost always get my equipment in when I need to."

Despite the lower yields, by 1995 his crops returned as much net profit per acre (including fallowed acres) as they had in 1989—the last year he used conventional "best management practices" before beginning organic management techniques.

With the right tools, healthy soil and well integrated weed management strategies, Erisman sees a much smaller role for herbicides and pre-plant tillage on sustainable farms in the future. ■

Brothers perfect disking, cultivating that beats no-till on sloping land

Glenn and Rex Spray
Mount Vernon, Ohio
- *500 acres* • *corn, soybeans, small grains, hay* • *disk tillage (30 percent residue)*
- *red clover cover crop*

Weed management highlights

Strategies: delayed planting into warm soil... crop rotation... high-tilth soil with increasing organic matter... mechanical controls

Tools: spike-tooth harrow... standard rotary hoe... four-row low-residue cultivators... rolling shields... tent shields

Two Ohio brothers understand the adverse impact of tillage on soil but demonstrate how a four-crop rotation helps them actually *build* soil on their rolling crop acres. Data from a nearby USDA research station and calculations from a county corn yield contest illustrate their system even beats many no-till systems in production and soil protection. (See "Disking down clover secures sloping soil," page 111.)

Mechanical weed control has been routine for more than two decades on the farms of Glenn and Rex Spray, two of Ohio's organic-farming pioneers. Their fields are made up of more than a dozen soil types with some bottom land, many hills and some slopes exceeding 7 percent. They plant their steepest fields to erosion-prone soybeans only in years when soil conditions are suitable.

Their soil-building cornerstone is a cover crop of KENLAND red clover, which they grow the season before they plant a corn crop. They value KENLAND (a certified variety of medium red clover) for its vigorous germination and growth. The legume is "frost seeded" by broadcasting into wheat or spelt from late February to April at about 8 pounds per acre. The first clover growth after grain harvest becomes hay for beef cattle, with the regrowth left for seed

harvest of 1 to 4 bushels per acre in late August.

Two fall passes with a 12-foot offset disk with notched blades kills the clover and incorporates some of the residue to start decomposition. A drag harrow added on the second pass smoothes the surface enough for winter application of about 8 tons of straw-pack beef manure. In spring, one or two diskings may be necessary to incorporate the manure, with two or three passes of a **field cultivator** with flat, 8-inch sweeps to kill successive flushes of weeds.

From pre-plant disking to canopy (when crop leaves shade out weeds between rows) is when the Sprays' row-crop fields have the least protection against erosion. Yet their corn ground readily absorbs water because it is soft, loose and spongy, the direct result of the previous year's red clover.

The brothers say that this soil condition is the key that allows them to use simple weed-control methods with simple tools, including

- **Spike-tooth trailer harrow.** This is the first tool into their fields after the planter. They use the harrow just as corn "spikes" at about 1 inch tall and before preemergent soybeans reach the brittle "crook" stage. The Sprays set their 24-foot, trailer-type McFarlane **harrow** to work in the top three-fourths-inch of soil. "A harrow moves 100 percent of the soil and disturbs every germinating weed, while a **rotary hoe** sometimes seems more limited to poking. It seems to depend on the year which works best," says Rex.

• **Re-pointed rotary hoe.** Within 3 to 10 days after harrowing, the Sprays are back in their fields when corn is about 1.5 inches tall with their 16-foot rigid-frame John Deere **standard rotary hoe.** Rex recommends getting in a quick second pass after breaking up a crust—later the same day or the next day—to prevent any germinating seeds from surviving in small chunks of the crust. "This will do you more good than waiting a week," he says.

When they needed a rotary hoe, they purchased a rebuilt unit because it had been fully outfitted with Ho-Bit **replacement spoons.** These hardened metal points are welded onto the ends of rotary hoe wheel arms to rejuvenate worn tips. "They're properly aggressive and well worth the money," says Glenn. In their loosest soils, they raise the three-point hitch a bit to keep the hoe from running more than about 2 inches deep.

After soybeans are well rooted—at about the two-leaf stage—he advises farmers not to worry about damage from the spinning fingers. "Truth is, you couldn't thin established soybeans with a rotary hoe if you wanted to," he says.

• **Shielded cultivators.** Front-mount, four-row straight-shank IH conventional **low-residue cultivators** work well on their sloping land where the rows are often contoured—but so would a newer six-row unit if its addition wouldn't require so many other equipment changes. They mount three or four 8-inch sweeps in front, followed by spring teeth on a rear toolbar to cover wheel tracks. The first cultivation is critical to a crop's success in relation to weeds, Rex explains. "If you don't get weeds on this round, you won't get them the next time, either." Running shallow—right through the root zone—when weeds are young increases chances

for success, he says. The brothers keep inside sweeps 3 to 4 inches from the row for all passes. Cultivating speed on first pass is a slow 2 to 3 mph to protect young plants but 6 to 7 mph on second pass to move soil into the crop row.

Round rolling shields and custom-built metal **tent shields** protect young crops and allow faster operating speeds. Adjusting the shields upwards allows loose soil to "flow like water" around the base of the plants while residue and soil lumps slide over the top.

The Sprays waited in '95 for warm soil for the same reasons as does Carmen Fernholz. (See page 41.) After planting corn in mid-May, they encountered the situation that skeptics of mechanical weed control cite most often—rain and cool temperatures. They first entered fields two weeks after planting to cultivate, when corn was 4 to 5 inches tall.

"Things cleaned up better than we expected," Glenn says. "Foxtail was a minor problem, but something in the weather must have suppressed the broadleaf weeds. The fields looked at least as good as usual."

Reports from the Knox Soil and Water Conservation District Corn and Soybean contest for three seasons show the Sprays' no-herbicide, no-fertilizer fields have out-performed many well-managed no-till fields.

While their yields of up to 175 bu/A usually rank in the middle third of the participating farms, the Sprays observe their profit per acre has been far greater than the other contestants. They cite two reasons: lower production costs and premium prices from customers who value top-quality, certified-organic commodities.

The four-year rotation of alternate grass and legume crops is their foundation for productivity, soil health, insect control and weed management. "This organic farming is mostly just common sense. Keeping ahead of weeds is really our biggest challenge." ∎

Guided precision tools finesse whole fields faster

Gary Thacker
County Extension Agent and researcher
Tucson, Arizona
• *Thacker developed prototype combination implement to increase cultivation efficiency* • *Coordinated on-farm trials and loans of prototype throughout Arizona's 400,000 acres of cotton*

Weed management highlights

Strategies: Cultivation-based weed control in commercial irrigated cotton... reduced herbicide use

Tools: In-row weeding tools (vegetable knives, crescent hoes, Bezzerides tools) mounted on a heavy-duty, straight-shank cultivator equipped with an articulated automatic guidance system

Arizona cotton farmers with high-residue cultivators equipped with in-row tools and a precision guidance system find they can cover more acres per hour and kill more weeds than with the cultivator alone.

Guidance accessories that keep cultivator units aligned with the crop row increase operating speeds, while in-row tools lightly work soil next to and even between crop plants. Combining these options on a strong single-sweep cultivator greatly expands mechanical weed management capacity, reports Gary W. Thacker, an Extension agent for agriculture in Pima County, Arizona.

He uses two types of tools from the Bezzerides line to uproot in-row weed seedlings. **Torsion weeders** are light, stiff steel rods mounted with a flexing loop base, and **spring hoe weeders** are flat steel springs. (See horticultural tool section, page 58.)

Both devices use a pair of opposing arms, each arm working alongside and lightly pushing against one side of the row area just beneath the soil surface. Spring tension allows the arms to uproot weed seedlings between plants but move around well-developed crop stalks.

Torsion weeders, which are able to move vertically to conform with the soil contour, are gentler than the more aggressive spring hoes, Thacker

reports. He says both tools can control in-row weeds in 4-inch-tall upland cotton—plants too small to withstand the impact of flowing soil moved into the row from cultivators or disks during the customary "dirting" to smother weeds.

He mounts a pair of these in-row weeders as the third of four soil-engaging tools on a heavy-duty, **maximum-residue cultivator** or straight shank cultivator. First comes **disk hillers** set 3 inches on either side of the row to cut and throw residue from the row area.

Next he knocks out weeds and sedges in the area between the disk-hiller swath and the outside edge of the crop plants. He's used **crescent hoes**—thin tines that curve at right angles to the row direction—to shear off weeds within 1.5 inches of the row. Thacker aims tips inward to the row, rather than the customary outward orientation, to reach under larger cotton plants. Gauge wheels must control the depth of the tool to keep it above seeding depth and away from plant roots, he notes. The crescent hoes also break up the smooth, firmed soil wall left by the disk hiller, allowing the trailing in-row weeders to work more effectively in loose soil.

Beet knives (also known as **vegetable knives** or delta knives) work even better than the hoes in this role, he discovered in '96. These are one-piece attachments resembling a half-sweep with a vertical fastening plate and a single thin, flat arm. Thacker also mounted these tools to run outside-in, running the trailing tip within 1.5 inches of the row. He emphasizes that adjusting to even minor row-width variation from planter to cultivator is critical in this type of ultra-close cultivation.

Only a narrow 1- to 2-inch bridge of soil in the row remains undisturbed after the initial tools pass. The in-row weeders described above pass through the soil next to crumble this strip, uprooting young weeds without disturbing rigid cotton stems. "Large cotton can tolerate very aggressive in-row weeding, which will kill virtually all weed seedlings and even some larger weeds," Thacker says.

Spyders™ (curved-tooth wheels bent from plate steel)—a third type of tool from Bezzerides—can run ahead of the in-row tools to break up the soil surface, but don't work as well as **disk hillers** to clear the way through tough patches of Bermudagrass or nutsedge, Thacker reports. He runs 14-inch, **one-piece sweeps** in the row middles.

He can manually steer the rig at about 3 mph, but cruises at 5 mph or more when he uses a Buffalo Scout **articulated electro-hydraulic guidance system.** He can cover 8 to 10 acres per hour with his six-row rig as the in-row tools and sweeps snuff out virtually all weeds across the swath.

Cotton plants can withstand aggressive in-row weeding once they reach the "pinhead square" stage at about 8 inches tall. "You see the plants wiggle when the rods nudge the stalk just below the surface, but they're fine—as long as you run shallow enough to avoid cutting feeder roots."

Thacker demonstrates his high-speed, multi-tool rig on the road throughout Arizona cotton country. Farmers watch it work and see its potential to cut their weed management costs. One grower said, "My hoeing crew costs $1,000 a day. This machine will cut that expense in half."

Editor's Note: Gary Thacker resigned his Extension post to start Pegasus Machinery Co. of Tucson, Ariz. The firm manufactures a one-pass implement that Thacker helped to develop to bury unchopped cotton stalks as it reforms beds. ■

Single-sweep shines in Georgia cotton

Nelson Hattaway
Blakely, Georgia
• *1,500 acres cotton* • *700 acres peanuts* • *oats as cover crop* • *strip tillage*

Weed management highlights
Strategies: Banding in-row herbicides... cultivators for escape weeds in row middles... winter cover crops... full-rate herbicides

Tools: single-sweep, maximum-residue cultivator... low-residue cultivator

Mechanical cultivation never went out of style in southwest Georgia, but a surge of interest in single-sweep, heavy-duty cultivators followed the advent of no-till cotton in the early '90s.

"Even where I haven't got much residue, my Buffalo 6300 keeps straight going down the row," says Nelson Hattaway. The **high-residue cultivator**'s rigid single sweeps travel through in his hard, red clay soils better than his S-tine multi-sweep. He uses the older unit, however, for repeat passes in severe weed infestations, and for herbicide banding. It's equipped with a gauge wheel for each gang of three sweeps.

The heavy-duty Buffalo cultivator with its residue-cutting coulter earns its pay, especially in slicing easily through heavy debris and patches of nutgrass that used to plug Hattaway's rolling cultivator. "The single no-till sweep basically takes care of anything in its path," he's found after two years of using it. He reports his units (he bought a second eight-row a year after the first one) work effectively without plugging, even in wet soils.

Hattaway runs 24-inch, **single-piece sweeps** between rows that are 36 inches apart. He runs **disk hillers** to within 6 inches of the row on his first pass in cotton and within 4 inches of peanuts. He keeps **flat-panel crop shields** on for all cultivations to prevent loose soil from interfering with herbicide in the crop rows (called the "drill" in cotton country). His challenging weeds include morning-glory species, nutsedge, buffalo grass, coffee weed and sand bur.

Hattaway fall-plants oats—at 2 bushels per acre, drilled in 7-inch rows, then harrowed lightly—to protect his soil and keep down winter weeds. He chemically burns down the cover crop when it's 6 to 10 inches tall. This is usually late March or early April, about a month before he strip-till plants cotton. He uses a six-row KMC no-till planter with residue-cutting coulters, heavy subsoiler shanks, fluted coulters, row-openers, gauge wheels and a soil crumbler roller ahead of a seeder unit. Seed is placed in a tilled, firmed and leveled 8- to 12-inch strip. (See Kelley Mfg. Co. in "Tool Sources" section.)

Hattaway bands a grass and broadleaf herbicide mixture over the foot-wide tilled strip at planting and broadcasts a second mix postemergence. He's still improving parts of the system but observes that it works best under irrigation so he can be sure to stimulate seeds and activate herbicides.

While hand-hoeing weeds is seldom done in his area, Hattaway wants to learn more about in-row mechanical weeding tools. "If it kills weeds," he admits, "I'm open to about anything." ■

Steel, flames beat back weeds in delta cotton

Steve McKaskle
Kennett, Missouri
- *1,100 acres (600 farmed organically)* • *sandy loam soil, Mississippi delta*
- *crops: cotton, soybeans, spelt* • *covers: grain rye, hairy vetch, buckwheat*

Weed management highlights

Strategies: crop rotation... composting and cover crops to improve soil quality... aggressive mechanical weed control... manual hoeing

Tools: "do-all" combination tool... standard rotary hoe... no-till cultivators... flamer

As a pioneer in managing cotton weeds without herbicides, Steve McKaskle quickly learned that change was going to be a central part of his management plan. Since '90 he has adopted new farming styles, crops and even colors of cotton in his quest for greater sustainability in the "far north" of the Mississippi Delta cotton country, just across the river from northern Tennessee.

McKaskle focuses on lowering weed competition at planting in his successful but evolving herbicide-free system. He uses organic methods on 600 of his 1,100 acres, relying heavily on tillage then flaming to manage weeds during the season.

His weed containment for the next year starts even before the current year's crop is harvested. Before leaf drop in cotton and soybeans, he seeds a grain/legume cover-crop mix at 63 pounds per acre (18 pounds of hairy vetch, 45 pounds of rye) from an airplane. "Having the seed mixed in a fertilizer blender and trucked directly to the airport is the secret to making this work," reports McKaskle.

He figures his air-seeding cost at about $4 per acre, considerably less than planting and disking passes by tractor. Falling leaves cover the seeds to create a moisture-holding mulch that enhances germination for a winter-long, weed-smothering, green carpet.

He gets an even earlier start for the coming year where he harvests winter grain crops of spelt or wheat in early summer. He immediately incorporates residue with two or three successive diskings, then uses summer-fallow tillage to attack weed patches. His fallow tool of choice is a Triple K. The high-speed tool features four ranks of 18-inch **S-tine cultivator** shanks outfitted with 4-inch sweeps ahead of rolling basket harrows. He runs it 2 to 3 inches deep at 6 to 7 mph before weeds reach 4 inches tall.

He avoids anything but shallow treatments until the following spring to conserve moisture. McKaskle makes an exception in areas infested with Bermudagrass. There he uses a chisel plow with 8-inch sweeps to expose the grass's roots to wind and intense summer sunlight. In persistent spots, he'll make a final run just before he expects a killing frost. The fallowed fields may handle an August buckwheat smother crop (drilled in 7-inch rows) that's harvested in October before receiving an overwintering rye/vetch or wheat/vetch mix seeded from the air.

By early April, the vetch is usually 12 to 18 inches tall, but biomass amounts vary with the winter weather. "Growth was thick as a hedge" after a mild winter in '95, but was thin in '96 due to cold temperatures, McKaskle reports.

Because of the importance of beds to hasten soil warming and retain deep moisture through the season, he goes through a series of tillage steps between winter cover and summer planting.

He incorporates the biomass by moldboard plowing 6 to 8 inches deep, then disking. A disk bedder is his tool of choice to create 38-inch wide beds that he then subsoils exactly where tap roots will need water. To do this, a "ripper/hipper" creates a shaft of loosened soil as it reshapes raised beds and prepares a flat seedbed to capture rainfall.

McKaskle's soil warms more slowly than the soil farther south, where much more cotton is grown. He waits for a predicted run of warm nights when soil temperature is 60°F to 65°F— usually two to three weeks later than neighboring farmers plant. His goal is to have germination within five days, giving his cotton a jump on weeds and a vigorous, competitive nature.

Cotton growers face a weed threat for about three months, compared with the six weeks it takes for Midwestern soybeans to canopy in 30-inch rows or for Midwestern corn to reach lay by (the point at which stalk height prevents further cultivation). This long period in his no-chemical program means McKaskle's post-plant tool treatments are critical to the crop's success.

The moment cotton plants reach 2 inches tall, McKaskle begins the first of two or three rotary hoeings. He starts with maximum down pressure on his **standard rotary hoe**—two springs hooked on his eight-row John Deere, 22-foot folding unit—releasing one of the springs if too many cotton plants are being plucked out. Crop roots are 2 to 3 inches long at this stage. To get the most out of the tool, he replaces hoe wheels that run on the beds each year. He operates the hoe about 2 inches deep at 6 to 7 mph.

McKaskle makes at least two rotary hoe passes, switching directions each time. These early runs are important to keep morning-glory, cocklebur, yellow nutsedge, teaweed (prickly sida or *Sida spinosa*) and "prickly careless weed" (*Amaranthus spinosus*) in check.

Soon after the crop is 3 inches tall, McKaskle's most accurate tractor driver begins cultivating at 2 to 3 mph. One of the last IH conventional **low-residue cultivators** made, McKaskle's unit came with five curved, spring-loaded shanks per row. He replaces the shanks next to the row with round standards. These he retools and adjusts to suit each phase of cotton weeding. He runs overlapping 10-inch, **medium-profile sweeps** in the row middles. The slight elevation in the center of the sweep mixes in more residue than would a low-profile sweep.

"We've run delta **(vegetable) knives** within two inches of the row, but I want to set **disk hillers** even closer," he says. He anticipated a bed-hugging **mechanical guidance system** he planned to add in '97 would make such an unforgiving margin possible. The knives have a thin vertical fin next to the row and a slim trailing arm that extends into the inter-row area.

"The disks can shave closer to the rows, and cut up vines better than the knives," McKaskle explains. He also wants a tool to work later in the season. It needs to have a positive slicing action that can knock out 2-feet-tall escaped weeds which the sweeps can't reach without damaging cotton roots.

Thanks to his crop rotation, cover crops and liberal use of composted cotton-gin trash, the sandy soil in his organic fields is loose but has a good tilthy softness from the added organic matter. Sweeps and knives pass cleanly through soil close to the crop without disrupting the plants in the "drill" (row area). Small weeds are easily dislodged and their roots exposed to the deadly drying effects of sun and wind.

When cotton reaches 6 inches to a foot tall, the operator increases speed and adjusts tooling to start "dirting the row," or throwing soil around the base of the plants. Weekly cultivations continue as long as needed, complemented by one comprehensive hand-hoeing after first cultivation and usually one quick walk-through to cut out final escapes.

In 1995, McKaskle figures he spent from 1.5 to 3 times as much ($50 to $75 per acre) for hand-hoeing in his organic cotton as in his conventional field, but still netted at least $100 more per acre, thanks to savings on other inputs and organic market premiums. He wants to test weed thresholds by species on his farm. Results will show if he can tolerate higher numbers of less-competitive weeds, or ones that do not quickly go to seed.

When cotton is 18 inches tall, McKaskle begins to use a **standard toolbar flame weeder** to manage in-row weeds. He attaches a 200-gallon, highway-certified propane tank to an old preemerge spray rig equipped with foot slides on angling runners. Two vaporizing burners per row fixed at 4 to 6 inches above the ground are angled to direct flame across the row area, one from each side. The burners are staggered so the flames don't collide and thrust upward into the plant. "You've got to have the flame going through the row to get a clean kill," he explains. "Keep the soil smooth so the flames don't bounce up into the crop."

At about $4 per acre, the flamer creates an efficient—if noisy—way to zap late-season weeds without tillage. (See "Hot Tips for Flame Weeding," page 27.) This type of flaming is a local pre-herbicide tradition that many conventional cotton growers are reviving to cut costs, save labor and master their toughest weeds, such as morning-glory. "Nothing is as effective as flaming once cotton is two feet tall," he explains.

With a minimum of new tools and skillful use of existing ones, McKaskle is dedicated to refining his integrated weed management system of cover crops, steel and flame. He wants more precise tractor driving to take out weeds closer and faster, and better flaming management to extend its use. Those changes should help him toward his long-term goals to reduce tillage passes and suppress in-row weeds even better. ■

II. HORTICULTURAL CROPS

The Tools

The economics of weed management are strikingly different in "high-value crops" than they are in larger fields of soybeans or grain. With gross income of more than $1,000 per acre, some tools make sense for vegetables or fruit that don't in a 200-acre corn field grossing less than half that much.

Yet costs are "high-value," too. Growers often need virtually weed-free fields for efficient harvesting. Weeds missed at early stages may cost $600 to $2,000 per acre to hand-weed later. Several aspects of vegetable systems favor cultivation:

• Tools for shallow cultivation in clean fields are lighter and less expensive than those that have to handle residue or move more soil.

• Irrigation allows "pre-watering" that sprouts surface weed seeds so they can be flame weeded or cultivated. This is a popular application of the "stale seed bed" technique. Tractor passes for reforming irrigation furrows or to use "crust busters" (rolling basket harrows run between rows) provide a cultivation opportunity without added tractor time.

• Well-made raised beds (to improve row drainage), with uniform shape and straight alignment, can be the cornerstone for efficient planting and cultivating passes. Bed sleds and cone guide wheels provide accurate guidance for planters and cultivators simply by hugging the bed sides. They are inexpensive to buy and operate.

Intensive crop rotations make herbicide use more troublesome in vegetable crops than in field crops. But that same complexity can be daunting to a grower investigating greater reliance on mechanical weed control. The grower may need to buy several unfamiliar implements, then learn how to operate, maintain, calibrate and adjust them to suit variable field conditions and plant sizes. To be effective, all the tools have to run "in synch," with some quite close to the row.

Once weed prevention steps begin to reduce weed pressure, basic vegetable implements can quickly pay their way in reduced labor costs. To get the most from these weed-fighters

• Simplify row spacing and bed width to minimize adjustments.

• Make sure each crop's income covers its need for specialized weed-control steps.

• Select tools you can alter to work at many depths, widths or crop sizes.

• Visit farmers to see how they create or adapt tools to kill more weeds with fewer trips.

In-the-row tools work well in loose, fairly dry soil without large clods or rocks. When used effectively, they can pre-empt tedious in-row hand weeding. Keep in mind the speed and residue limitations of these tools.

Specialized tractors for cultivating were made through the '70s. They had offset seats and engines to improve the operator's view of the center row, and usually had higher clearance. "Cultivator tractors" like the Allis G have a rear-mount engine and an open front frame design. See the Appendix for locator lists.

Also used in vegetable fields and orchards are "broadcast tillage" tools such as harrows and rotary hoes (see Section I), and the disk harrow and field cultivator, presented in Section III.

Spyders™ ▶

Used in pairs to crumble soil and dislodge weeds close to row; alone or immediately ahead of in-row weeding tools. Each ground-driven, 12"-diameter wheel of quarter-inch steel has 16 offset teeth mounted on a ball-bearing hub. Wheels can be positioned on the toolbar to push soil in or switched to pull away soil from the row, or swiveled to work a narrow or wide band.

When set with the leading edges pointing outward, the wheels squeeze and crumble the soil surface between them in the row area. Recommended operating speed: 4 to 5 mph.

Price: $150 per set, with standards

Source: 14   **See:** Foster, Thacker

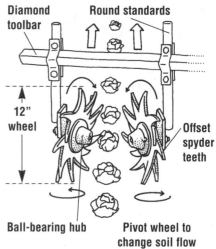

◀ Torsion weeders

Square tines of 3/8" steel used in pairs, mounted on either side of the row and angling downward and back toward the row. Coiled base allows tips to flex with soil contours and around established crop plants, uprooting weeds in the white-root stage within the row. Usually follow Sypders™, sweeps or crustbreakers for greater precision. Similar to a "Texas rod weeder."

Price: $74 per set, with standards

Source: 14

See: Foster , Thacker

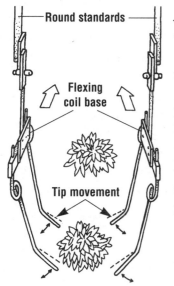

Spring hoe weeders ▶

Paired sets of elongated, 10-gauge metal plates that kill small weeds (up to 1") by slightly moving the soil between crop plants in the row. More aggressive than torsion weeders, made from flat spring steel that flexes and vibrates next to the row just below the soil surface. Usually follow Sypders™, sweeps or crustbreakers for greater precision.

Price: $96 per set, with standards

Source: 14   **See:** Thacker

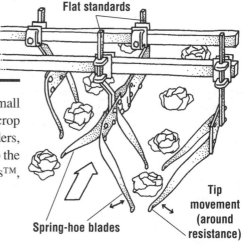

Finger weeder

Overview: Steel cone wheels—rotated by ground-driven spike tines—push rubber "fingers" just below the soil surface, reaching into the row. Fingers can work safely in the row in crops that have sufficient stem strength and root resistance, such as corn, strawberries, nursery stock. Tool dislodges small weeds (up to 1") only; operating depth 0.5" to 0.75". Works best in loose soils, and will not work in heavily crusted soils or where long stemmed residue is present. Usually "belly mounted" under motor block, but can be mounted on three-point rear hitch, or on outriggers for split-row coverage in nursery use.

Two pairs of finger cone wheels run in sequence, followed by a pair of bent-tine mulching cone wheels. The finger wheels tilt downward so that the rubber fingers hit the soil at an oblique angle. Set the leading finger wheels about 1" further apart than the rear ones. On stiff-stemmed crops, the second set can be positioned to have fingers overlap one-half inch for total in-row coverage. More tender plants need greater distance to prevent crop damage. Multiple row units require 36" between rows.

Design Features: Eighteen flexible rubber fingers 3.5" long radiate from 7" metal hubs. Angle and adjustment determine aggressiveness of action. Springs cushion impact by obstructions. Rigid frame requires level bed for best results.

▶ **Model for comparison:** one-row, two sets of finger cones, one set mulching cones
  Rec. PTO HP: 25   **Speed:** 3 to 6 mph   **List price:** $800

Width range (all makers/all models): 1 to 2 rows

Source: 19, 65   **Farmers:** Harlow, Muller

CROP height range estimate

| 0" | 2" | 4" | 6" | 8" | 10" | 12" | 18" | 24" | 30" | 36" |

WEED height range (annuals) estimate

■ suitable   ▨ less suitable   □ unsuitable

Crop canopy shape affects tool's ability to safely reach the stem. Match tillage timing, depth and location to crop root growth. Weed control varies with soil conditions and weed density.

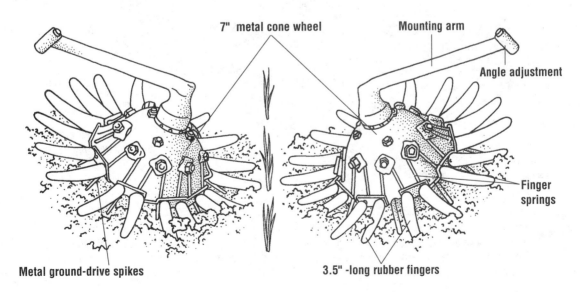

7" metal cone wheel · Mounting arm · Angle adjustment · Finger springs · Metal ground-drive spikes · 3.5"-long rubber fingers

Basket weeder

Overview: Rolling baskets made of quarter-inch spring wire thoroughly weed the top inch of soil without moving soil into the crop row. Works only with small weeds in soil that is friable and not crusted, and cannot handle long-stemmed residue. One of better tools for emergency weeding in moist soils with minimal clay content. Units are custom-made as to basket width (2" to 14"), axle width and mounting positions. Flat (bed-top), slant (bed sides), angled (row hills) and offset (for extra-wide spacing overlap) basket shapes can be configured to meet many field conditions. Telescoping center baskets provide the ability to cover a varying width—e.g., as crops grow to make the between-row area narrower—by increasing or decreasing the degree of overlap. Baskets can be adjusted to overlap and used for broadcast cultivation with no crop present.

CROP height range estimate

0"	2"	4"	6"	8"	10"	12"	18"	24"	30"	36"

WEED height range (annuals) estimate

suitable   less suitable   unsuitable

Match tillage timing, depth and location to crop root growth. Weed control varies with soil conditions and weed density.

Design Features: Baskets 13.5" diameter and of various widths are mounted the width of the unit on a square axle. A chain connects a gear on the front axle with a smaller gear on the rear axle set back about 20", rotating the rear baskets at a faster rate for a more aggressive mulching and aerating effect.

▶ **Model for comparison:** three crop rows on a 40" bed
  Rec. PTO HP: 30   **Speed:** 4 to 8 mph   **List price:** $600

Width range (all makers/all models): 1 to 18 rows

Source: 19 (K series), 65   **Farmers:** Gemme, Harlow

Mounting frame

Ground-driven weeding baskets

2X gearing spins rear shaft

TIP: For more aggressive action in a broadcast application in raised beds, find a section of a spiral bar rolling incorporator. These are often used as finishing or residue incorporating rollers behind a field cultivator or chisel plow. Belly mounted, a 4-foot section can be an excellent, low-cost, high-speed way to kill flushes of small weeds on a bed under stale seedbed management.

Multiple-component weeding frame

Overview: This flexible unit performs many weeding tasks on wide-row or bedded vegetable crops. Its precision furrow-following guidance system holds tools within 1" of the row, using guide wheels in the furrow or guide cones that hug the shoulders of raised beds. It can be used as a broadcast-tillage weeder before germination, and then in a row-crop mode with sweeps, spiders (offset-tooth wheels) or other tools attached to front or rear weeder toolbars.

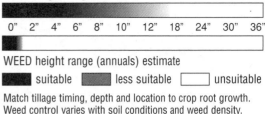

CROP height range estimate

| 0" | 2" | 4" | 6" | 8" | 10" | 12" | 18" | 24" | 30" | 36" |

WEED height range (annuals) estimate

■ suitable   ▨ less suitable   ☐ unsuitable

Match tillage timing, depth and location to crop root growth. Weed control varies with soil conditions and weed density.

Design Features: The tool is designed around a flex-tine weeder 50" wide housed in a sturdy frame. It is wide enough to cultivate wheel tracks on either side of 40" beds. By lifting up tines over the row and keeping them out of the way, he can work around crops up to 16" tall. The dual toolbars allow precision weeding tools solidly fastened on diamond clamps to work close to the row, or between plants, while the tines work the middles.

▶ **Model for comparison:** 50" weeder, front and rear diamond toolbars (2" square), steel disk guide wheels, gauge wheels, track sweeps, spiders
   Rec. PTO HP: 50   **Speed:** 3 to 5 mph   **List price:** $3,845

Source: 65

Options: additional toolbars on rear (if rear gauge wheels used for support); shanks for knives, sweeps or in-row tools

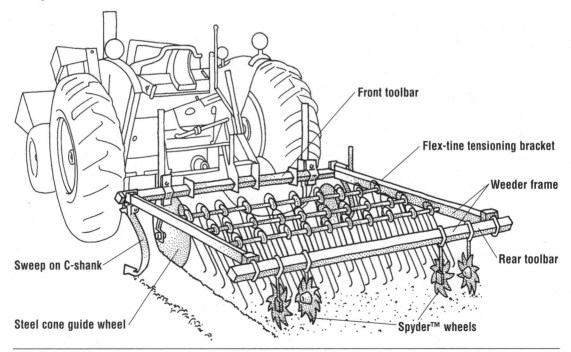

Front toolbar

Flex-tine tensioning bracket

Weeder frame

Rear toolbar

Spyder™ wheels

Sweep on C-shank

Steel cone guide wheel

Brush weeder

CROP height range estimate

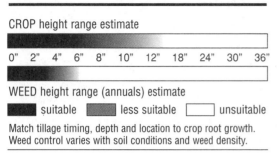

| 0" | 2" | 4" | 6" | 8" | 10" | 12" | 18" | 24" | 30" | 36" |

WEED height range (annuals) estimate

▇ suitable   ▨ less suitable   ☐ unsuitable

Match tillage timing, depth and location to crop root growth.
Weed control varies with soil conditions and weed density.

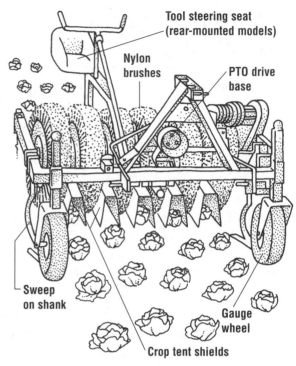

Tool steering seat
(rear-mounted models)

Nylon
brushes

PTO drive
base

Sweep
on shank

Gauge
wheel

Crop tent shields

Overview: Vertical brush weeders use rotating nylon bristles to pull weeds and aerate soil about 1" deep. Rapidly spinning bristles turn in the direction of travel and run between the rows. The bristles penetrate the soil crust as they pull and shred weeds. The flexible bristles don't create compaction, but leave worked soil as a fluffy mulch that helps to regulate soil moisture. Usable in any soil moisture level where a tractor can be reasonably driven; less effective in hard, dry soil conditions.

Design Features: Metal crop shields (2" to almost 5" wide) protect crops from moving soil. Brushes 20" or 30" in diameter and at least 4.75" wide are custom built to till a specific width of inter-row area. The smaller version can be belly mounted or rear-mounted, while the larger diameter hoe must be rear-mounted. Brushes resemble a section of a street sweeper brush and are PTO-powered. Parallel linkage on each brush maintains consistent depth on uneven terrain. Rear mounting requires a second person (who sits behind the brushes) for precision steering.

Note: Horizontally rotating brush hoes use pairs of much smaller brushes on either side of a row. They use hydraulic, battery-electric or PTO power. The brushes resemble a household vacuum cleaner's circular brush attachment. They can be tractor-mounted or horse-drawn to cultivate up to five rows, or set on manually pushed tool carts for single-row application. Tubular steel carts use off-road bicycle wheels. Useful in moist soil. (Horizontal hoe sources, both Scandanavian: 30, 94)

▶ **Model for comparison:** 72" toolbar, 6 vertical brushes (20" diameter) for 5 rows
  Rec. PTO HP: 30   **Speed:** 1 to 3 mph   **List price:** $5,000
  Only 72" toolbar; brush/shield configuration made to order.

Sources: 8, 94

Farmers: Brush weeders are currently used more widely in Europe due to stringent herbicide restrictions there. Relatively few are used in North America outside of forestry nurseries. Robin Bellinder at Cornell University (see "Contacts," p. 118) recorded several years' experience with a vertical brush hoe and other leading European tools in vegetable systems.

Backpack flamer

(wand type)

Overview: These portable units are intended for spot weed control or stale seedbed coverage on limited acreage. They require at least modest physical strength but weigh less than 25 pounds. Regular 30" wands work for reaching weeds near one's feet. Extended wands allow the operator to reach across a row to flame weeds in adjacent rows, or to angle flame away from the buried edge of a row's plastic mulch.

Design Features: The units include backpack frame, regulator, hose and burner. Fuel cylinders may not be included. Cylinders range from 11- to 20-pound capacity (about 4 pounds per gallon). Standard gas grill tank is about 18 pound capacity. Regulators available to adjust flame intensity.

List Price: $70 to $100 for kits of gas-delivery components, excluding backpack and cylinder; $240 to $350 for complete units.

Use described: deWilde, Muller   **Sources:** 33, 45, 77, 98

CROP height range estimate

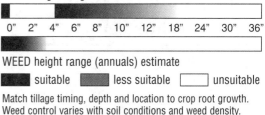

0"   2"   4"   6"   8"   10"   12"   18"   24"   30"   36"

WEED height range (annuals) estimate

■ suitable   ▨ less suitable   ☐ unsuitable

Match tillage timing, depth and location to crop root growth. Weed control varies with soil conditions and weed density.

LP cylinder (11-pound) — Regulator

Backpack frame

Extended wand

Backpack flamer

(wheeled manifold)

Overview: Commercial market gardeners without tractors can flame stale seedbeds over a substantial area with this tool. Operator pushes from walkway for raised beds, or between beds in flat fields. Works close to plants developed enough to tolerate indirect heat from flame.

Design Features: The 2' housing holds four 2" torches and concentrates their heat across its width. One model adjusts for height and features a 1" diameter stainless steel frame.

List Price: Two models, $225 and $250; regulator $50; tanks and backpack frame purchased locally.

Source: 28

Also: see toolbar flamer, page 29.

CROP height range estimate

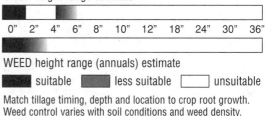

0"   2"   4"   6"   8"   10"   12"   18"   24"   30"   36"

WEED height range (annuals) estimate

■ suitable   ▨ less suitable   ☐ unsuitable

Match tillage timing, depth and location to crop root growth. Weed control varies with soil conditions and weed density.

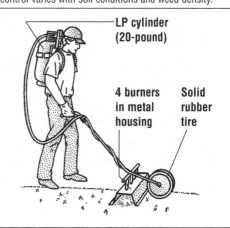

LP cylinder (20-pound)

4 burners in metal housing

Solid rubber tire

Rotary tilling cultivators (multiple heads)

CROP height range estimate

0"	2"	4"	6"	8"	10"	12"	18"	24"	30"	36"

WEED height range (annuals) estimate

■ suitable　▨ less suitable　□ unsuitable

Match tillage timing, depth and location to crop root growth. Weed control varies with soil conditions and weed density.

Overview: The spaces between their independent gangs and their vertical clearance of 18" to 24" allow weeding in many crops long into the season. Metal housing around the tilling blades protects plants and contains moving soil. These tools are designed and constructed for shallow tillage—high-speed slicing of weeds just below the soil surface—not primary tillage. They can handle less crop residue than the solid-shaft tillers and are lower priced. Depending on soil and residue conditions, the better multiple-head units work for strip-till planting if suitable seedboxes are cushioned from vibration to allow consistent seed placement.

When working young plants in crusted soils, tiller cultivators tend to decrease clodding compared with sweep cultivators. Because sweeps need to be driven slowly to avoid pushing clods onto the plants, the tillers can travel faster in these conditions, do a superior job of weed control and cause less crop damage. Overall, tillers can work effectively in moister soils than can sweeps.

Design Features: The individually suspended inter-row gangs are mounted with parallel linkage; heads vary in width from 5" to 60" by knife width and arrangement. Gangs attach to a main toolbar. Chain drive powers the heads from an elevated hex-shaped PTO drive shaft that runs parallel to—and just below—the main toolbar. Heavy-duty models have cast-iron gearboxes. Some makers provide two lengths of chain housing for better adaptation for use on raised beds. Additional furrower attachments are necessary to move soil into rows for any in-row weed control.

▶ **Model for comparison:** 66" to 72" wide; working three 18" rows on 60" bed
Rec. PTO HP: 25 to 35　**Speed:** 2.5 to 5 mph　**List price:** $4,500 to $6,300

Width range (all makers/all models): 1' to 18'

Sources: 11, 32, 65 ,72, 99　**Farmers:** Berning, Haines, Harlow, Kenagy

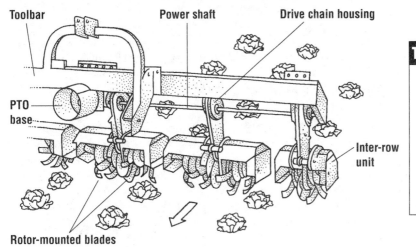

Toolbar　Power shaft　Drive chain housing

PTO base

Inter-row unit

Rotor-mounted blades

TIP: For small market garden farmers, a walk-behind tiller can serve as an effective shallow cultivator if properly set. High vertical sides limit how close these units can cultivate to the row of a crop with a broad canopy. Sources: Ardisam, BCS, Garden Way, Goldoni, Snapper

Rotary tillers (convertible to cultivating)

CROP height range estimate

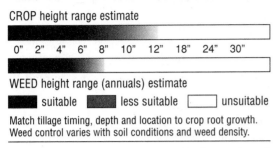

0" 2" 4" 6" 8" 10" 12" 18" 24" 30"

WEED height range (annuals) estimate

██ suitable   ▓▓ less suitable   ☐ unsuitable

Match tillage timing, depth and location to crop root growth.
Weed control varies with soil conditions and weed density.

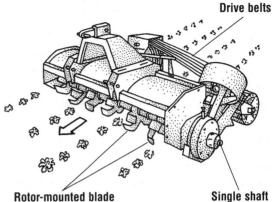

Drive belts

Rotor-mounted blade   **Single shaft**

Overview: Rotary tillers have blades anchored on rotors that are bolted directly to a single horizontal power shaft that is 8" to 12" above the soil surface. For row-crop weeding they are more expensive and require more maintenance compared with sweep cultivators. They can be operated faster than sweeps in crusted soil, but would be slower in normal conditions. However, tillers are more adaptable to other tillage roles and may reduce field passes by incorporating residue, forming beds and creating a seed bed in a single pass. Uses include strip-planting into cover crops, preparing permanent planting beds, renovating strawberry plantings and incorporating compost or soil-applied herbicides. Blade length limits the height of the crop that will pass unharmed under the solid drive shaft. Visibility of the working area limited by tool cover.

Design Features: Rotors must be selectively removed or adjusted to do inter-row weeding—at least a two-hour job. Drive shaft is PTO-powered by chain drive in most cases. One manufacturer's multiple-belt drive cushions sudden impacts. Features to check include multi-speed gearbox drive (slowest RPMs prevent soil structure damage), PTO slip clutch for chain-drive models, and depth-control mode. When working rough soils, front depth-gauge wheels don't provide as even a job as side skids or a rear crumbler/roller. Optional crop shields keep soil from flowing into row.

Blade shape varies the tool's effect. Slightly curved "C" or angled straight blades pass most easily through heavy residue, moist soils and deeper levels. "L" blades have a 90-degree bend and wide horizontal cutting surface for shallow undercutting of vegetation—with minimal incorporation. Blade strength, type of metal used and number of blades per rotor will influence value, effectiveness and durability.

▶ **Model for comparison:** 15' toolbar working six, 30" rows (6R30)
   Rec. PTO HP: 120 to 150   **Speed:** 1 to 6 mph   **List price:** $14,000 to $35,000

Width range (all makers/all models): 6' to 30'

Sources: 5, 31, 75   **Farmers:** Berning

TIP: Rule of thumb—Estimated power requirement for rotary tillers is 7 to 10 PTO horsepower per working foot for strip-tilling or cultivating.

Retracting tree weeder

0"	2"	4"	6"	8"	10"	12"	18"	24"	30"	36"

WEED height range estimate (with stiff-tined weeding head)

▇ suitable   ▓ less suitable   ☐ unsuitable

Match tillage timing, depth and location to crop root growth.
Weed control varies with soil conditions and weed density.

Overview: These units use passive tooling or active tiller heads to cultivate between trees or staked vines. As the implement moves along the row, the tool retracts into the row-middle area as a sensor contacts the tree or stake. Some makers offer one or more fixed-position shank mountings for sweeps, shovels, subsoilers or barring-off disks close to the moving head. Others design rugged tool carriers compatible with the moving part.

Design Features: In automatic units, a hydraulic sensing arm contact triggers the retraction, with the tool moving back into the row when the obstruction has been passed. These units are usually mounted onto the right side motor block or rear three-point hitch. Manually controlled units allow for more varied control. An alternative pivoting version can be front-, side-, or rear-mounted or attached to the side of a between-the-row toolbar cultivator.

Options: Self-contained hydraulic systems power active tillage heads. On-the-go tilt control gives operator more control in variable orchard conditions. Rear-mount, three-point hitch wrap-forward units place the head within the view of the operator, similar to the side-mount unit shown here.

▶ **Model for comparison:** rotary tillage head with coiled-base vertical tines
   Rec. PTO HP: 18 (with auxiliary hydraulic power) and up; 30 to 80 for PTO drive
   Speed: 1.5 to 4 mph   **List price:** $3,000 (manual retraction) to $7,500 (automatic)

Sources: 14, 38, 40, 50, 60, 99, 101

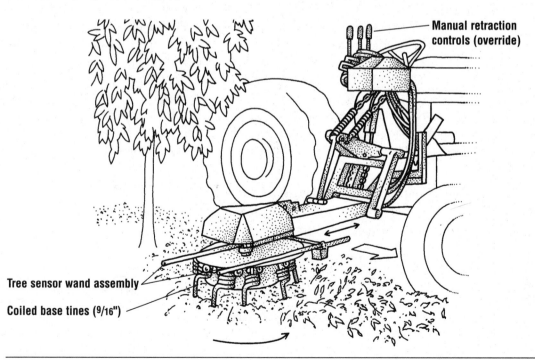

Manual retraction controls (override)

Tree sensor wand assembly

Coiled base tines (9/16")

Horticultural Crops: The Farmers

Diversified Oregon grower matches tools to the task

Bill Chambers
Corvallis, Oregon
- *1,300 acres* • *sandy loams to silty clay loam soils* • *grass and sugar beets for seed* • *38 inches precipitation annually, dry summers*
- *wheat; squash/pumpkins, sweet corn and broccoli for processing*

Weed management highlights

Strategies: crop rotation (irrigated and non-irrigated, early- and late-seeded)... cover crops to suppress weeds... modified stale seedbed tillage-cultivation-planting sequence... hand-hoeing

Tools: flex-tine weeder... rolling cultivator... rotary power harrow... high-residue cultivator... low-residue cultivator... sweeps, disks, tines and shanks to mix and match as conditions require

Bill Chambers isn't alone when planning weed management strategies for his vegetables, sugar beets, wheat and grass seedstock at Stallbush Island Farm. He has crop specialists and mechanics on staff to watch conditions and respond with appropriate tool combinations. But it's Chambers who brings an economist's rigor to redesigning whole-farm cropping systems that optimize on-farm resources and get more from his weed-killing tools.

Chambers evaluates the long-term costs and benefits of steel tools and cultural practices, calculating maintenance, labor and crop niches. He uses virtually all of his weed management tools for several rotation situations—another way that crop diversity works in his favor. He has abundant farm labor to hand-weed pumpkins, a practice which keeps field clean, pumpkins healthy, soil pesticide-free and wages circulating in his community.

He already raises broccoli, sweet corn and pumpkins without herbicides and is decreasing his dependence on the sprays wherever else he can. Driving his quest for new strategies and tools is a nearly empty chemical arsenal, as there are few herbicides still labeled for use in his crops. "In pumpkins, I had one broadleaf label and two grass herbicides," he explains. "They're designed to work in Midwest weather and Midwest soils. They don't always work here and they're very expensive. So alternatives pay."

He rotates the moisture cycle on each field, irrigating for two years then farming dryland style for one. His crop sequence is sugar beets for seed, pumpkins, sweet corn, perennial ryegrass for seed, broccoli, pumpkins then wheat or grass for seed. He sometimes substitutes snap beans for broccoli. Chambers uses grass/legume cover crop mixes. His main one is oats planted at 60 pounds per acre with common vetch (*Vicia sativa* L.) at 30 pounds per acre as soon as possible following previous crops.

To kill the covers in the April 10 to May 10 window, he flail mows the cover within 1.5 to 2 inches of the ground, then waits about 30 days before he begins tillage. Dry matter deposited by the covers is about 7,500 pounds per acre. If he doesn't have at least two weeks to allow the residue to break down, he will use Roundup herbicide.

A favorite tool is his 30-foot **Lely flex-tine weeder,** which resembles a light, high framed harrow and works as a light broadcast cultivation tool. The four ranks of coiled tines—each about the diameter of a thin pencil and 15 inches long—rake the soil surface to pull out and expose sprouting and emerging weeds. He waits until crops are established well enough to survive some tissue damage. He uses a 70-hp tractor which gives good stability and control on moderately flat fields.

Chambers had only read about the weeder when he bought his model in 1993. He quickly realized how well it would fit into his operation.

He runs the weeder preemerge diagonally over fields seeded with sweet corn and pumpkins fairly fast—"as fast as you can hang on is fine." He goes through again as needed, driving more slowly up and down the rows once crops have three or four true leaves. "This time, you have to get off, get down next to the row and look carefully at the crop," he says. He adjusts tractor speed, coil tension and tine depth to kill weeds but protect the crop. The Lely's tines work best when weeds are in the vulnerable white-root stage, *before* they have any true leaves.

Chambers says each operator has to develop a "gut instinct" for what constitutes tolerable crop damage by the tines. "Sweet corn plants are fine if the growing point is undamaged, despite torn leaves. Pumpkins can take a lot higher damage than you think," he has found. "In some passes I feared that I had reduced plant population by 25 percent, but a week later you couldn't tell I'd been through." His target weeds in pumpkins are sow thistle, redroot pigweed, nightshade and shepherd's purse.

He's learned not to disturb pumpkin seedlings for a 10-day period after germination. The plant is brittle and vulnerable in this stage. Once it reaches the three-leaf stage, it is robust

"I'm in transition from a chemical-intensive system to a management intensive system that's more sustainable—but also more demanding."—Bill Chambers

enough to lose a leaf and keep growing. He can knock out up to 15 percent of the young plants with no yield penalty. Pumpkins, like soybeans, have a compensatory growth cushion provided by extra growth of the neighboring plants.

The Lely and other flex-tine weeders designed for row crops have individually retractable tines. Chambers uses this feature when he cultivates growing broccoli and sugarbeets, lifting tines up over the row and away from contact with the tender plants. He sometimes runs into trouble, however, in the sugarbeets because of differences in germination between pollinator and seed rows that demand different settings for best weed control close to the row.

He later bought a second, smaller 15-foot Lely weeder for postemergent weeding. The narrower width improves the evenness of penetration in his river-bottom fields, which have swails up to 15 feet deep. Both his weeders have gauge wheels to help even out penetration from side to side of the tool. It takes almost a year for beets to set seed, requiring continuous weed management. His tine weeder cuts one—and sometimes two—herbicide applications from the traditional three-spray crop. Control of volunteer vetch, wild oats, Canada thistle and catchweed bedstraw are critical to produce high-quality, weed seed-free beet seed. Volunteer grains and well-rooted grasses are tough early competitors that often survive the weeder, he cautions. He cleans up these weeds while the beets are in a dormant phase by broadcasting a herbicide mix or by hand hoeing minor infestations. He adds 2 pounds of boron per acre to enhance the herbicide action.

Chambers has tried using the Lely weeder postemergence in winter wheat. To avoid disease pressure in wheel tracks due to compressed soil, he waits until after the first freeze to plant. It takes a "tricky dance with the weather" to seed then weed the newly emerged grain crop before winter rains set in.

Other tools he uses are

• Box-beam cultivator toolbar (4 inches square, 15 feet long) and an array of steel weeding tool choices—narrow points for maximum penetration, **wide sweeps** for undercutting the surface, **cutaway disks** large and small to move soil away from or toward the row, **Lilliston rolling cultivator** spider gangs, subsoiler points to remove tire tracks and **duckfoot sweeps** to combine good soil entry and surface action.

• Bi-directional, 90-hp Ford 276 tractor. Seated facing the cab end and driving down the row cab-end forward gives him the visibility advantages and immediate turning response of a mid-mount tool. "By looking right into a tool that I'm pushing forward, I get instant feedback so I can make faster decisions," Chambers says. He travels 4 to 5 mph.

• Lely Roterra rotary harrow. Designed as a PTO-powered secondary tillage tool, the Roterra works well to eliminate weeds and loosen soil where a well-tilled seedbed is needed. It uses pairs of sturdy vertical club tines 9 to 11 inches tall to stir the soil by spinning horizontally. The tops of the tines are mounted to a round base secured in series across the width of a flat-frame gearbox.

Chambers uses the Roterra to prepare soil for all crops except his covers and is careful to replace tines and other moving parts each 7,500 acres of use—about once every three years for him, given the Stallbush Farm's multiple passes and crops.

• IH 140 offset, high-clearance tractor. The 30-hp tractor—built for cultivation—has its engine offset to the left and a frame for belly-mounting cultivators between the front and rear axles, in front of the driver. Chambers uses the vintage mid-'50s tractor to run cultivators up to 10 feet wide. He stays in fairly flat fields because the rigid mount shanks have limited ability to flex over uneven terrain.

Chambers wants to take computer-assisted optical pattern recognition technology now used for pinpoint herbicide spraying and apply it to mechanical weed control. He's working on an in-row, up-and-down sweep assembly that will travel between pumpkin rows, raise up quickly upon reaching a pumpkin plant, then quickly drop back down. The software will be able to distinguish between green leafy weeds and green leafy pumpkins, a job that now only humans can do.

"I spend about $32,000 a year for weed control in pumpkins—400 acres at $80 dollars per acre in a weedy season," Chambers explains. A machine that reduces his costs by two thirds would provide $21,312 in annual savings. Capitalizing the purchase over five years at 8 percent would allow him to spend $85,000 for the tool, he calculates.

That's high-priced steel by traditional standards, but it illustrates Chambers' commitment to his "computer analogy" of weed control systems. He likens the toolbar and tractor to the electronic hardware, while sweeps, knives and tines are the software that the operator has to knowledgeably select, configure and apply. Without a deep understanding of soils, crops, and costs, a farmer will be at a loss to make even the right tool compute. ■

Flaming, close cultivation, cover crops control Wisconsin vegetable weeds

Rich de Wilde
Viroqua, Wisconsin

- *40 acres* • *cover crops: oats, winter peas, hairy vetch, red clover*
- *silty loam soils* • *30-inch bed plantings, single or double row per bed*
- *fresh-market vegetables: salad greens, onions, garlic, snap beans, root crops* • *cut flowers*

Weed management highlights

Strategies: crop rotation (planting location, time of season)... cover crops to break weed cycles... mechanical and thermal controls... hand-hoeing... stale seedbed with tillage and flaming

Tools: toolbar flamer... hand-held flamer... frame combination weeder... rotary hoe... light disk

Insight: "I've learned the importance of faithful rotations. Two years of salad greens set me up for a chickweed explosion in September of the third year, so I seeded an extra-thick stand of oats and peas. It suppressed the chickweed, winterkilled and broke down easily the next spring."—*Rich de Wilde*

Rich de Wilde plants, nurtures and harvests 40 acres of specialty greens and vegetables, emphasizing novel varieties and crop diversity. He's as deliberate and innovative in managing weeds with steel and flame as he's been in helping to build demand for premium quality organic produce in the Upper Midwest.

That doesn't translate into a lot of high-priced machinery or commercial technology. Instead it means he focuses his management skills on integrating shallow tillage, cover crops, stale-seedbed planting and crop rotation with precision cultivation and aggressive, carefully delivered and well-timed flaming. By successfully lowering weed pressure each year that he farms a field, he cuts costs and labor devoted to weed management—adding dollars to his bottom line.

De Wilde follows the advice of his tobacco-farming neighbors. "They said to never let weeds go to seed. We've stuck to that rule for the 11 years we've been here. And we've noticed that our fields have gotten incredibly cleaner. There's a lot less hand-weeding to do now."

He plugs a clean hand-weeding into his budget at $360 per acre—60 hours at $6 per hour. It's a treatment of last resort, but one that's justified because of its immediate and long-term benefits. That striking cost figure helps him critically evaluate other approaches that meet his personal goal—and his organic certification mandate—of a no-herbicide system. It also motivates his early season management.

Another piece of his organic approach is to optimize a broad range of nutrient levels based on lab tests of soil samples. Optimum fertility tied to crop needs gives crops early vigor to outcompete weeds. This strategy is especially important for the direct-seeding he finds most efficient for small-seeded crops. De Wilde believes that his attention to applying calcium, sulfur and trace minerals has added to the crops' advantage.

He uses a moldboard plow 4 to 6 inches deep every two or three years of the crop rotation to incorporate a rank cover crop of rye, hairy vetch and red clover, but chisel plows 8 inches deep for primary tillage whenever possible. Limiting pre-plant tillage to the top several inches minimizes how many weed seeds are stimulated by movement and light. When the first flush of weeds sprouts in a week or so, he makes a pass with a combination of a light disk or cultipacker and steel drag. He repeats the pass if he has to wait for a second flush to emerge.

His frequent but low-impact tillage sequences do not cause surface compaction of his silt loam soils. He subsoils 18 to 20 inches deep in alternate years to maintain excellent percolation and root-zone looseness.

Within this context of intensive weed suppression, de Wilde works with flaming and cultivation to kill small weeds. Applying flame broadcast—across the entire soil surface—just before the crops emerge gives them a tremendous advantage. De Wilde uses a **toolbar mounted propane unit** with four liquid gas, self vaporizing burners mounted on an old cultivator frame. He can set the burners to provide a solid wall of flame, or angle two burners per row to hit only at the base of crop plants once heat-tolerant crops are mature enough. He needs only a $9/16$-inch wrench to adjust pivot attachments that connect the burners to round pipe standards.

Preemergent flaming is especially effective for slow germinating crops such as onions, parsnips, spring carrots and larkspur, a flower which he plants for fresh cut sales at farmers markets. Weeds are so problematic on superslow developing parsnips, de Wilde says, that he wouldn't consider raising them without a flamer.

To cut the interval between flaming and crop emergence as short as possible, de Wilde uses market garden expert Eliot Coleman's "window method." A pane of glass placed over the seedrow causes a crop to germinate about two days early—usually enough time to check the weather and set the last "safe" time to flame the row before the tender crop seedlings emerge.

Flaming after crops emerge is an option that demands carefully adjusted tools and a more skilled operator. De Wilde recalls a field of garlic where patches of purslane in 6-inch rosettes became a problem within the row. He had already cultivated, but the rolled-in soil had failed to stifle the succulent weeds. Without a span of hot, dry weather, de Wilde knew that even hand-pulled purslane turned roots-up could survive to haunt him again.

He cranked up pressure on his gas regulator to 45 psi (compared with his usual pressure of 35 psi) and slowed down tractor speed to about 2.5 miles per hour (compared with his top flaming speed of 4.5 mph). Bulb reserves helped the singed garlic leaves to rejuvenate. The shallow-rooted purslane died. Other growers report purslane is nearly immune to flaming, and also often survives sweep cultivating.

Much like the postemergent use of a rotary hoe, what the operator sees happening during flaming is not the final result, i.e., crop damage isn't as severe as it looks. Unless he's confident of what flaming will do in a particular situation, de Wilde spot tests with a hand held burner (one with a flame equivalent to his row crop flamer) before he treats a whole field. Determining on-the-spot if weeds will die and the crop will live is a critical acquired skill. (See "Hot Tips For Flame Weeding, page 27.")

Any flame contact on the growing point or leaves of a crop is likely to set back growth. Growers get the benefit of flaming without losing crop productivity by applying it via stale seedbed, with crop shields or with water-spray shielding.

De Wilde recalls with chagrin a learning moment with a test patch in a field of potatoes early in his flaming career. Only a few green sprouts had emerged, and trauma to the young leaves within the flamed area seemed too severe to him to withstand the treatment. When he returned 10 days later, the flamed part of the field had vigorous, weed-free spuds. The rest of the acre had to be hand-weeded. His misreading of the leaves cost him many hours of labor.

Potatoes are unusually vigorous in compensating regrowth after leaf loss thanks to the stored energy in the "seed" tuber.

The staggered plantings of a diversified vegetable farm require de Wilde to manage weeds under many different situations. While he doesn't have the degree of control that flood irrigation gives dryland growers, he has found that flaming works best in the hottest parts of the hottest days of summer. He hits this window when he puts in fall carrots. That sequence is soil prep (chisel plow and disking), a week's wait for weed-seed germination, flaming to eliminate sprouted weeds, then seeding with the least possible soil disturbance.

"Propane is nice and clean—in the field, in our greenhouse furnaces and in our forklift," de Wilde says. "I treat it with great respect, and I've had no problems safety-wise. I'm still working on my management and my nerve, but that's about knowing when the flame is too hot or too close for my crops."

He calculates that flame weeding costs him $10 to $12 per acre for fuel, labor and equipment. A forklift-type LP gas cylinder covers about 2.5 acres. At 2.5 mph, he can flame-weed onions (double rows on 30-inch beds) at a rate of a half-acre per hour.

When he needs gentle cultivation for young small seeded crops, de Wilde turns to a vintage Italian combination frame weeder he found at a Michigan used-machinery yard. Central to the weeder's precision is a frame that rides on the ground. De Wilde replaced its skid runners with 4-inch wheels. Tooling includes vegetable side knives, 7-inch sweeps and small 4-inch cutaway disks. De Wilde added curved round metal fingers that run in front of the disks at ground level to nudge tiny plants to an upright position, out of reach of the disks. He adjusts the disk to run 0.50 to 0.75 inches deep and about 2 inches from a row of plants at least 2 inches tall. Driving this tool is a demanding job. "It takes a really good person who's really awake," de Wilde reports.

"I set the disks at a slight angle away from the row so they just scratch out about a one-inch band next to the row," de Wilde explains. "The side-knives come down the middle of that furrow so that the trailing arms smooth out the outside edge." He keeps the knives sharp and runs them flat and shallow to minimize soil movement into the row.

This is a precision, clean-tillage tool that depends on the flat surface created by a smooth roller pulled over the rows after planting in a separate pass. The uniform flatness puts the growing points of each weed closer to the same level, increasing the effectiveness of the knives. "When rain keeps the roller out, it's a nightmare to cultivate," de Wilde reports. When things go well, the roller/combination-weeder sequence cuts hand-weeding in half.

But this farmer wasn't satisfied. To beef up his anti-weed tool squad, de Wilde next fabricated an extendable, belly-mount, two-row cultivator mounted on an International Harvester (IH) Super A. The tractor's offset opening ahead of the driver gives an unobstructed, straight-ahead view of tools working the soil.

His Super A is for cultivating—period. Many commercial market-farmers have one or several tractors just for cultivating, often with the same implement permanently mounted and adjusted, to get the right steel in the field at the right time. He also outfits the tractor with a conventional low-residue, multiple-sweep cultivator with straight shanks and 2-inch shovels. In '96 he bought an IH 140 offset tractor and married it to his Italian cultivator.

De Wilde knows weeds will always be around, daring farmers to manage them. By containing weed pressure through preventing new weed seed whenever possible and suppressing weed competition through stale seedbed preparation, de Wilde is confident that his close-in cultivating and finely-tuned flaming will keep the stragglers in check. ■

Confidence in postemergence flaming comes with experience, innovation

Phil Foster
Hollister, California
- *200 acres (buried drip, sprinkle irrigation)* • *fresh vegetables*
- *clay soils and sandy loam soils* • *certified organic* • *cabbage, peppers, fennel, celery, sweet corn, melons, hard squash, garlic, onions*

Weed management highlights

Strategies: cultivation... flaming... pre-irrigation... transplanting... cover crops... hand weeding... crop rotation

Tools: low-residue cultivators... precision bed tooling... homemade guidance sled... toolbar flamer... torsion rod in-row weeders... rolling cultivator... disk hillers

Experience is a great confidence builder, and it takes lots of confidence to subject a field of high-value garlic to the cell-bursting heat of a flame weeder. Phil Foster has done it often enough that he feels comfortable seeing blackened greens as he pulls from the field. He knows that the garlic will come back but that the current crop of weeds is history.

His farms include clay (3 to 4 percent organic matter) and sandy loam soils (1.5 percent organic matter) and receive 12 to 13 inches of precipitation annually, mostly from December to March. Careful use of furrow, drip and sprinkle irrigation systems keeps crops green. He uses pre-irrigation to encourage a flush of weeds that he lightly tills out prior to planting—a traditional dryland practice widely used by many farmers, conventional and organic. Running a single, permanent drip line deep below crop rows lets him limit weed growth by concentrating water close to the crop roots. Through careful use of a mechanical spader, he can even till in a cover crop with the drip lines in place.

Foster builds beds that are 40 inches wide and about 5 inches tall to plant a broad mix of vegetable crops in a year-round growing season.

Cover crops improve and protect his soils.

Covers include a cereal grain (rye, wheat or barley), Magnus field peas or a mixture of vetch (purple or lana woolypod), peas, bellbeans and oats. Ahead of planting, he flail mows the cover crops then incorporates them with a spading machine or offset disk with 24-inch blades.

He applies carefully managed, often-turned compost produced on his farm to increase fertility and biological activity in soil. The major application—about half a field's yearly total—goes on in the fall to prepare for fall and winter planting. He applies from 9 to 12 tons of compost per acre per year. Even after a cover crop, he applies 5 tons per acre to continue building soil quality.

Preemergence flaming is Foster's most efficient early season weed control. He uses a two-bed toolbar mounted flamer, which has four burners per bed. He orients burners pointing backward, parallel to the direction of the rows. This prevents small weeds from being protected from the flame by the indentation left by packer wheels. Weed escapes in this groove are more likely when flames shoot across from the side.

He concentrates on flaming *before* crops emerge to purge the seedbed of living weeds, but he uses postemergent heat treatments as he gains experience with timing. Field patches with heavy weed pressure, or fields that didn't receive proper early season control, are post-emergent candidates. He estimates he's flamed about 10 per cent of his acres per year post-emerge over the last decade.

Foster considers postemergent flaming as a rescue strategy. In onions, he calculates a 10 to 15 percent production loss from the treatment, which sets the crop back about 7 to 10 days. The effect on onions is more pronounced than on garlic because onions are day-length sensitive, he explains. And onions planted toward the end of the planting window will suffer most in final bulb size.

To make a postemergent decision, he estimates weed pressure. If it looks like it would cost more than $500 per acre to clean up by hand-hoeing, he brings in the flamer.

In '95, he had 7 acres of yellow storage onions at the two- to three-leaf stage. Threatening were lambsquarters, pigweed and malva (dwarf mallow) as cotyledons and 1-inch rosettes. "Flaming knocked out a big portion of the weeds, saved me at least $500 in labor, and still gave me a good yield," he recalls. "I got as many onions as from a neighboring non-flamed field that had lower weed pressure."

Flaming garlic may take two passes—one preemerge and a second, if needed, by the time the tallest plants hit the three-leaf stage. Foster's garlic emerges more variably than his onions. This means 20 percent of the plants may be at the one-leaf stage while the most mature plants have three. The leaves are most likely to burn back, but they will regrow, he says.

Foster has increased flaming field speed over the years to 3.5 to 4.5 mph, using 10 to 15 gallons of propane per acre. At $0.90 per gallon, that's $9 to $14.50 per acre per pass for the fuel.

He removed hoods from the flamer when he added the second set of burners, but kept vertical side metal panels (that resemble cultivator crop shields) mounted on adjustable standards.

"You could put on a top hood, but I like to see the burners during operation."

Shields keep the flames from being directed away from weeds by stiff breezes that are common during the afternoon "prime kill time" of maximum air temperature and dew-free weeds.

Foster finds that transplanting more than pays for its extra field labor and greenhouse costs, thanks to full season savings in managing weeds and insects. The stronger, older plants are better able to fend off both types of pests. He transplants such crops as lettuce and cabbage, as well as crops with especially expensive seed such as hybrid pepper, hybrid cabbage and seedless watermelon. He cultivates transplants as soon as they are well-rooted enough to withstand a gentle wave of soil pushed in by sweeps from between the rows to smother in-row weeds.

Where soil is loose and flows well, a mechanically guided cultivator and straight rows give him good enough control to cultivate with only a 3-inch band for the row. A farm-fabricated guidance sled holds the 8-foot toolbar in place. The V-shaped structure of angle iron rides in a single furrow between the two or four beds being worked, locking the cultivator in alignment. Foster loosens sway bars on flat fields so the tool can easily follow the guide, but tightens them up on slopes where the mass of the sled may pull downhill.

His four-row bed shaper makes it possible to use either his two-row or four-row cultivators, both with sled guidance. He covers 0.66 to 1 acre per hour with the two-row unit and about 2.5 acres per hour with the four-row.

His onion **cultivator** is a farm-fabricated model with bed-top **vegetable knives** running along the outside edge of the outside rows. Five-inch-wide **duckfoot sweeps** cover the inter-row areas. He runs these tools within 1.5 inches of the onions where soil is friable and clod-free, a condition he attributes at least in part to his regular addition of compost.

His in-row, paired Texas-style rod weeders (**torsion bar weeder**) let him lightly disturb loose soil even closer to plants. The thin, round coil-mounted rods angle down from each side to almost meet tip-to-tip near the base of the crop.

His best success with a **Lilliston rolling cultivator** has been in sweet corn. He cultivates as soon as the crop is 3 to 4 inches tall, running slowly and with the curved tooth spider gangs set at a slight angle away from the rows. When the corn hits 10 inches tall, Foster pivots the spider gangs strongly the other direction to throw soil between the rows then travels at 4 mph or more.

In addition to their bed-top cleaning role, **vegetable knives** are his main tool for managing weeds in the wide inter-row areas in melon and squash plantings early in the season until vines shade the soil. He uses the knives and **disk hillers** to get close to plants and slice off weeds in the early season pass. The next weed flush is extinguished when he splits the vacant bed left between each planted bed. Shovels and disks push soil in both directions, creating 80-inch beds and smothering weeds along the outside edges of the planted beds.

When the vine crops begin to set runners, he makes a final pass with 12-inch top knives running as close as he can to the spreading plants. These long, bevelled straight knives run at right angles to the row just below the soil surface. He can offset about 6 inches of these knives in from the side and under the ends of the vines. The fast-spreading foliage takes over the weeding job after that.

When Foster has to cope with perennials such as morning-glory and Canada thistles in his long-season crops, he relies on cultivating with disks and knives for the sprouts up to 4 inches tall. After that size, the toughness of the plant prevents a clean kill, and handweeding becomes necessary. His goal is to prevent viable seed or root-mass from increasing the weed's threat to the field's next crops. ■

"Ancient" tooling runs fast and close to yield greens without weeds

Gary Gemme
South Deerfield, Massachusetts
- *100 acres* • *soils: coarse sand to silt loam* • *wholesale fresh vegetables*
- *conventional tillage with cover crops* • *limited herbicide use*
- *greens (beets, chard, collard, kale, mustard, turnip), tomatoes, peppers, eggplant*

Weed management highlights
Strategies: winter, summer cover crops (grains, legumes, grasses, mixes)... early precision cultivation of direct-seeded crops... on-farm greenhouse produces transplants to allow aggressive early cultivating... crop rotation... plastic mulch... preemergent herbicide on direct-seeded crops

Tools: basket weeder... belly-mount sweeps... rolling cultivator gangs... spring teeth

In 20 years of producing vegetables, Gary Gemme has invested much in weed control—much time and attention, that is, in building his management skills.

He's still perfecting the precision use of implements he bought or inherited with the farm. He minimizes hand labor through modest herbicide applications and timely use of old steel that works as well as anything else he's seen on the market.

Even paying himself $20 per hour for driving tractor, Gemme figures his mechanical weed control approach saves money compared with a heavier herbicide routine. In mostly pre-emergent applications, he applies labeled herbicides for collards, kale and peppers to give crops a jump on weeds. In all other growing situations, he depends on steel or occasional hand weeding.

Winter cover crops of rye, wheat or hairy vetch suppress weeds and protect his soil when they are green. They begin to build up soil organic matter when they are incorporated in spring. After subsoiling about 24 inches deep diagonally across the field, Gemme plows as carefully as possible to create an even, loose layer of topsoil. A soil rake (a single bar holding rigid tines) on the plow helps break up the soil, and he uses a light tandem disk as needed.

Whenever possible, he waits several weeks for the cover crop biomass to begin decomposing. He then forms 54-inch beds with sides about 4 inches tall. Furrows between them are 18 inches wide. Everything but the solanaceous crops (tomatoes, eggplant and peppers) is transplanted into the beds in three rows, 18 inches apart, centered on the bed. Tomatoes go in single rows, peppers and eggplant in double rows (staggered offset planting), all on 72-inch centers and usually with black plastic mulch.

His crop rotation for most fields is Year 1—brassicas (collards or kale); Year 2—solanaceous crops, beets or chard; Year 3—a summer soil-building crop such as sorghum-Sudangrass, a fast-growing and heat-loving annual. To create a five-year rotation between solanaceous plantings, he often sublets a field to another farmer to raise a suitable crop for a year, then returns to brassicas.

"No other cultivator I've used comes close to the Buddingh **basket weeder** when you've got a small flush of weeds in seedlings," says Gemme. Belly mounted on his Farmall Cub, he uses the tool in two ways. At the normal speed of 3 to 5 mph, he sets the wire baskets to within 3 inches of one another to cultivate young direct-seeded crops, such as onions. Gearing doubles the speed of the second set of baskets, giving them what he calls a sweeping motion that nicely mulches loose soil.

When he has taller transplants that may have a few small weeds in the row, he moves the baskets 4 inches apart and pulls back the tractor throttle. Cruising at up to 8 mph, he says the baskets *do* throw soil into the row—a use of the tool not intended by the manufacturer but cherished by this Massachusetts vegetable grower.

Because precision tools such as the baskets put steel quite close to crops, exact adjustment is a continuing part of tool management. "Things are set right when the baskets clip just a couple of leaves per row. If there's no contact, you can probably get a little closer," says Gemme. He sets the tractor's front wheels so their inside edges run against the outside edges of the bed, using the elevated soil as a no-cost guidance system. This combination works well on his flat, river bottom fields free of stones.

Gemme adds heavy wire tines ahead of the baskets to break up heavier soil for extra weed control. From his experience, he would not recommend the basket weeder for fields with rocks big enough to bend the basket wires; hard soil; frequently wet soil; crops with a wide, leafy canopy; or as primary control against grasses with rhizomes, such as nutsedge and quackgrass.

He's found the basket weeder can control weeds more than 1 inch tall if they are growing sparsely. In a thick patch of weeds, a half-inch tall is the safe maximum height. Except in especially flexible crops such as onions and garlic, he figures 9 inches is maximum crop height.

Because of their quick growth, Gemme's greens usually only need one more weed-control pass before the leaves make cultivating impossible. He uses 8-inch sweeps on a low-residue cultivator a week or two after the baskets. These are the now-standard "medium-profile" style, which have a moderate difference between the sweep's raised center area and its wings. It's tumbling action mixes surface residue with soil more than the "low-profile" style used in wider sweeps on the more rugged single-sweep cultivators.

During this final "lay-by" pass, his main mission is application of 40 to 50 pounds per acre of nitrogen fertilizer next to the rows, dribbled through tubes from two tractor-mounted hoppers. The late application is the key to top yields in the nutrient-hungry crop, he's found. Because some crops also need soil hilled to prevent lodging, Gemme figures dragging the cultivators is a virtually no-cost weed-control pass. For the record, his $8 sweeps last him about three years on a four-sweep set-up that cultivates about 100 acres per year.

He adjusts the sweep tips down (angling the sweeps ends up) and increases tractor speed in order to hill as much soil as possible at the base of plants. This avalanche of loose soil retains moisture and suppresses weeds within the rows.

When weed pressure is heavy, he may make two basket passes and two runs with the sweeps. Some weeds demand follow-through beyond the current crop. For instance, Gemme mentally notes areas of high galinsoga population during spring crops. After harvest, he tills then packs the soil to create ideal conditions for the weed. He subjects the area to a fallow period during summer heat, shallow tilling it repeatedly with his tandem disk just deep enough to kill the weeds. He believes a springtooth harrow or field cultivator would do the job even better.

This practice depletes surface weed seeds and readies the area for fall planting. He can seed a commercial crop of beet greens or Swiss chard before August 15, or cover crops of hairy vetch from late August through early September or rye until mid-October. Gemme transplants—

rather than direct-seeds—a spring crop into the area to maximize crop competition if the galinsoga should persist.

"I'm still working on the perfect system for controlling weeds that grow along side of plastic mulch, but I'm getting closer," says Gemme. His tools of choice to work in the difficult area adjacent to the buried plastic sheet edges are spider gangs, such as those found on a **Lilliston rolling cultivator.** He can angle the soil-chewing, curving spider wheel arms to cover the entire area between the rows of plastic mulch. Their angled, slicing entry into the soil takes out weeds close to the plastic. Gemme's spider gangs are his only "new" tools, purchased several years ago with his bed former.

He keeps a close watch on mid-season weeds, looking for signs that will tell him which tool he needs to use next. "Every tool has its weakness, and changing the combination each pass keeps weeds on the defensive," says Gemme. He still ends up with one hand-weeding per season of the plastic mulch. "Some weeds always grow in the center holes next to the crop, and there's some with roots right in the buried fold of the plastic."

He rotates "ancient" spring-shanks in his line-up, usually using them next to the plastic to pick out strips of weeds. "Nothing can get closer, and I can angle them if I have to," Gemme says.

Because "We're forever tearing cultivation tools off and re-installing other ones," he's hoping to add a second small "offset" tractor reserved for weed control. His current tractors are the Cub and a Farmall 200 (a 1957 version of the Super C).

As a category, offsets are general-use tractors of 10 to 30 hp. The engine section is moved to left of center and the seat rests next to the right fender. This realignment offers the driver an unobstructed view of the right half of the row area. (See "Specialty tractors for weed control," page 117.) Used models with gearing that allows extra-slow travel in small plants are especially valuable. Gemme is looking for a cultivating tractor with vertical clearance greater than the 14 inches on his Model 200, a non-offset model.

"Too often, we finish working a patch before we get the adjustment just where we want it," he explains. When a tool stays on a given tractor, it's field ready at a moment's notice. When there are crops to harvest, cultivate and plant before lunch, saving 15 minutes hitching time can be the difference between being in the field and just knowing you should be.

"In most of my soils, cultivating seems to stimulate plant growth," Gemme observes. "When my soils get sealed by rain and heat, plants don't thrive." But in fields with coarser sand, he accepts some extra weed pressure rather than risk additional moisture loss during dry periods. He cultivates only if he's sure he can follow with irrigation once the weeds are dead.

"Weeds are getting tougher," says Gemme. He's getting tougher on them, too, by learning their weak points and sharpening his weed-management strategies. ■

Flexible steel, dependable cover crops launch trials for organic no-till

Kenny Haines
Misty Morning Farms
Belvidere, North Carolina
- *200 acres* • *swamp and mineral soils* • *certified organic*
- *48-inch bedded rows* • *wholesale fresh market vegetables*
- *rye/vetch, summer covers*

Weed management highlights

Strategies: intensive early cultivation... cover crops... transplanting slow-growing crops

Tools: rotary tiller... flex-tine weeder... S-tine cultivator... rolling cultivator... vegetable knives (standard and reversed mounting)

Ten years after starting organic production on 10 acres, Kenny Haines is confident he can control weeds with a handful of tools and careful crop selection on 200 acres of widely varying soils. "If I can get in to cultivate, I don't have a problem with weeds," declares Haines.

He plants crops from March to October, usually establishing two vegetable crops and one or more cover crops per year in most fields. His packing shed supplies national organic chains with field crops of summer and winter squash, cucumbers, broccoli, cabbage, Brussel sprouts, carrots, sweet corn, peppers, tomatoes and snap beans. He extends production of tomatoes and cucumbers in greenhouses covering about two-thirds of an acre.

Because Haines can't control the area's frequent rainfall that encourages weeds in prepared soil, he waits until he can "freshen the beds" just hours before planting. When the interval between incorporating cover crops and forming the beds is short, he uses a bed shaper. Its flat metal panels rub against the top and sides of the bed, working the soil surface just enough to disrupt germinating weeds.

If beds are still well-shaped but weeds and

*"There's not one super-tool
or simple method to non-chemical
weed control."*— Kenny Haines.

grass are more developed, he adds ranks of **S-tine shanks** with 1- to 2-inch shovels over each bed. He mounts S-tines ahead of the shaper and uses a row of bed-firming straight minicoulters behind it to prepare the bed for planting.

When heavy rains pack and round off beds to the point where precision weeding would be difficult, Haines uses a **rotary tiller** with bed-shaping panels. His favored tool is a 6-foot Maschio tiller, which features a heavy-duty chain and structure that fits his needs better than a lighter KMC 19-foot model. His next tool to build will be a 16-foot, PTO-driven tiller to work three beds at a time.

The tiller will be part of his move to standardize row spacing to simplify integration of tillage, planting, cultivation and harvesting equipment. Many vegetable growers with more than 50 acres under production agree. Their calculations show they can realize long-term labor and machinery savings if they strategically upgrade from dissimilar row-width implements.

Haines plants as many crops as he can on 48-inch beds that are 72 inches on center, with 24-inch furrows.

"Planting" at Misty Morning Farm means transplanting for all vegetables except quick-spreading vine crops and sweet corn. Yet Haines uses the same weed control equipment whether crops start as seeds or sturdy seedlings. "We'll start using our 20-foot Lely **flex-tine weeder** within a few days of planting seeds, and as soon as transplants are firmly rooted—usually less than week," says Haines. He uses Speedling transplants, which have an inverted pyramid shaped root ball that provides added stability.

"The weeder works best before the weeds poke through, the same as a rotary hoe," he explains. He considered both tools before buying the Lely, basing his decision on the overall and individual-tine tension adjustability of the weeder and its longer operating window in terms of crop maturity. Broccoli plants up to 5 inches tall don't suffer from a weeding pass, he notes.

Haines loosens tension on the weeder's looped coil adjustment in his rich, soft swamp soils, which have up to 10 percent organic matter. The non-crusting soil flows easily around the thin round tines, giving the tool nearly ideal operating conditions.

On some of his rental ground, the light-framed Lely has difficulty aerating crusted mineral (clay) soils, even at its highest down-pressure setting. A second pass is required. The weeder's gauge wheels help to maintain a consistent tine depth. When he needs to protect crops as they get older, he takes 10 minutes to swing up tines over the nine rows (three beds) he weeds per pass.

He introduces three more types of steel— 5-inch sweeps, vegetable knives and rolling cultivator gangs—as weeds and crops develop. He achieves the best weed kill by mixing passive sweeps and knives—which move through the soil—with the greater shattering action of vibrating S-tines and the ground-driven rolling cultivator.

"Sometimes I'll see little weeds with their roots holding on to a ball of soil after I cultivate with my S tines," he explains. "The soil is loose, but the weeds can re-root. The Lely reaches any place across the bed to knock the roots loose so they dry out." He usually pulls the frame weeder at 6 to 8 mph—twice the S-tine's top speed. But when he has full-leafed weeds in his heavy soil, he needs the S-tines to break them loose first.

"There's not one super-tool or simple method to non-chemical weed control," Haines cautions. "My neighbors have an arsenal of herbicides. I need an arsenal of steel with pieces that roll, cut, and scratch the soil—whatever it needs."

He continues the dual-position use of **veg-**

---

etable knives that's been customary in his region for decades. On the **early cultivator passes,** he sets the knives with the upright fin next to the row and the single trailing arm angled back away from the row. The vertical steel fin shunts all soil away from the row, running within 2 inches of the crop.

"I run just as close as I can hold the tractor to the row," he explains. "Sure we lose a few plants, but I don't skimp on seed. It pays off in close-in weed control."

Hains constructed the cultivator frame for these tools in his shop. The main 4 x 7-inch tool-bar holds the typical round pipe gangs for rolling cultivators. At the rear of the pipe gangs are brackets for sweeps. He hangs the knives on a 4 x 4-inch secondary toolbar, which is attached 3 feet behind the main frame with channel iron.

On **later cultivator passes,** as crop plants bush out to create a canopy, he reverses knife positions. He moves the knife's toolbar attachment bracket so that the vertical fin runs far from the rows and the tip of the sweep slices to within inches of the crop stalks. The "tip-in" setting reaches under a canopy in a way few other tools can. Point-to-tip knife arm lengths range from 8 to 16 inches.

Rolling cultivator spider gangs make their biggest contribution in combination with the knives. The round standards and other adjustable brackets allow the spider gangs to be swiveled to control soil flow (toward or away from the row) and angled to the exact slope of the bed sides, uprooting weeds while maintaining the bed shape.

Haines likes the weed suppression and soil-building benefits of his winter cover-crop standby combination—rye and hairy vetch drilled at one bushel and 25 pounds per acre, respectively, following a light disking of the beds. He lets the cover grow in spring as long as he can to add biomass and nitrogen to the soil. The following crop

sets the actual tillage date—earlier for sweet corn, as late as rye heading-out stage for fall squash.

Haines uses a rotary tiller to incorporate the cover crop, a move that makes sense because of his need to create raised beds. The tiller does both jobs in a single pass. To seed cucumbers and squash, he attaches a planter to the rear toolbar to roll the three jobs into one.

He's confident that his work with summer covers such as millet, quick-growing clovers and flowering native species will give him new cropping options that will reduce tillage while he suppresses weeds, builds soil organic matter and creates habitat for beneficial insects. Flail-type stalk choppers to knock down covers, no-till transplanters and high-residue cultivators for weed control can open up new options for no-till, no-chemical vegetable systems. He sees niches in his system where buckwheat and soybeans will bridge spring and fall crops.

"We haven't even touched the tip of the iceberg in no-till vegetable production," Haines says with a sense of urgency. He knows his grandfather sowed red-top clover with turnip seed in front of a tine weeder,giving him a winter legume crop after the fall root harvest. Haines wants to synthesize that kind pre-fertilizer era wisdom with the best weed control practices and soil building strategies.

"If we think hard about the future, maybe we can pick up the knowledge we need from the old people before we bury them," he muses. "Farmers hear it the best from other farmers, and we need more of them to get to work with trying new ideas with covers and cultivators." ■

Grower shuts off weed windows before, after and between crops

Tom Harlow
Westminster, Vermont
- *50 acres in crop rotation* • *soils: sandy river bottom, gravelly clay*
- *fresh market vegetables, mostly wholesale* • *certified organic sweet corn,*
winter squash, short- and long-season greens, carrots, parsnips

Weed management highlights

Strategies: stale seedbed... specialized cultivation... crop rotation... handweeding...
winter cover crops

Tools: tandem disk... mid-mount cultivator... offset cultivator tractor... basket weeder...
in-row finger weeder... flamer... field cultivator... rolling cultivator

Detailed employee timesheets tell Tom Harlow *exactly* what it costs to produce each of his fresh vegetable crops each year. He drops the crops that don't pay, but says that harvest labor—not his steel-based weed management system—is usually the culprit.

He watches income closely from his high-labor root crops of parsnips and carrots. He wants to make sure that organic premiums balance out the timely, precision cultivation and hand-weeding costs that may hit $2,000 per acre. After eight years of fulfilling cropping standards to be a certified organic farmer, he's satisfied with his weed management system. "Sure I'm fine tuning things, but it's close to being just where I want it."

The weed species shift during his nine years of organic weed management bears him out. His annual tillage has fully suppressed perennials (troublesome witchgrass and sedges are gone), but opened up the niches for annuals such as chickweed and galinsoga. By matching competitive crops with weed pressure and rotating crops and tillage, he keeps these new opportunistic annuals—as well as the ever-present pigweed and lambsquarters—in check.

To build soil and keep winter-annual weeds contained, he plants winter covers of winter rye, or rye mixed with hairy vetch. He rotates greens, root crops, sweet corn or squash—with winter cover crops between each—then two to three years of red clover, sometimes harvested as hay and sometimes just clipped. This rotation mixes the type of crop root growth (shallow tap roots of greens, slender tuber of parsnips, radiating feeders of corn, and deep fibrous roots of clover) to prevent any weed species from developing a comfortable niche.

Harlow incorporates rye two ways. He uses a tandem disk with 22-inch blades on the fields he turns under earliest in the season, starting in late April. Later in the season, he uses a moldboard plow to handle more biomass from taller rye. His river bottom soils are not erosion prone, and the tillage improves their aeration and water infiltration. Until the fields are bedded, he kills weeds before they are an inch tall with brisk broadcast passes of his **tandem disk** or a **field cultivator** with barely overlapping 6-inch sweeps.

Next he forms beds that are 42 inches on center, elevated 3 inches higher than the 9-inch furrows between them. These become his "stale seedbed" sites where he works to deplete the weed seed bank in the top few inches of soil. He sacrifices the soil-building value of several weeks of cover crop growth to provide time for two or three cycles of weed growth.

Harlow fabricated a bed-top, spiral rolling harrow that uproots and disturbs weeds. He cut the high-speed tool from a spiral basket roller section of a large field cultivator, then fashioned a bracket so he could belly mount it on his John Deere HC900. He says the high clearance, offset tractor is perfect for his cultivating jobs. Visibility is excellent, the machine is maneuverable and it takes him only 10 minutes to change cultivators. Even if he didn't also use it to spray and sidedress fertilizers and flame weed, he believes it would still be worth "twice what I paid for it."

For the final weed-killing pass at the last possible moment before crop emergence (for direct-seeded crops) or transplanting, he uses a German LP gas bed **flamer.** Its shrouded burner manifold (roughly resembling a rectangular rotary mower housing) concentrates heat on the soil surface. Its fixed 40-inch width and burner positions limit the tool's use to "broadcast flaming" in a stale bed application.

The unit's six burners burn up $32 of LP gas per acre. Ground speed—and consequently, fuel use—-varies with conditions. Harlow travels about 6 mph on dry afternoons when weeds die more easily, but only 4 mph when he has to flame on dewy mornings. Harlow says his next flamer will be a standard U.S. toolbar version with targetable burners. He wants it to do broadcast flaming on beds of different widths, as well as banded flaming between rows of growing crops.

He plants most crops in two rows, each 9 inches from the bed center. Corn and collards go in 36-inch rows, and he direct seeds winter squash in rows 8 feet on center.

His most difficult weed challenge comes from his 2 acres of parsnips, a notoriously slow germinating crop. They take two to three weeks to come up and demand 100 growing days to produce their sweet white roots. His earliest planting requires that he compress his stale seedbed treatment, and the cool soils lengthen the time before the developing crop becomes competitive. The third planting in mid-July faces intense weed pressure at a time when labor for cultivation and hand weeding competes with early harvest of other crops. Harlow says he usually loses a fraction of the plantings to weeds but still turns a profit thanks to strong consumer demand and the unwillingness of other local growers to battle weeds in the crop as tenaciously as he does.

His root-crop strategy calls for a whole-bed flaming just as the earliest parsnips or carrots come through. When the crop has emerged and white-root weeds start to gain some color—and even reach up to a 2 inches height—Harlow runs through with a **basket weeder** (Buddingh Model H) within 1 inch of the row on either side. Its ground-driven heavy wire tined baskets roll horizontally against the soil surface to push through the soil and leave a mulch between the rows. No soil is thrown onto the weak parsnip seedlings.

Site selection to avoid patches of crabgrass is critical in turnips. With their growing centers well-rooted below ground, crabgrass plants survive scorched leaves from flaming and aren't killed by the shallow basket attack.

The next tools to protect the parsnips are the shanks of a belly-mount cultivator. Soil and weed conditions determine what soil-engaging tools Harlow mounts on the fixed vertical shanks. Shovels only 2 inches wide go deep when soil's been packed. Half-sweeps travel close to the row without moving soil toward it. These pieces have a sweep arm on only one side. They are usually mounted to extend into the middle row. Full sweeps 6 or 8 inches wide work the middles between rows and may throw soil in-row, depending on speed, proximity to the row and sweep profile.

After the first sweep cultivation, a hand-hoe pass removes all weeds in the parsnip patch, Harlow reports. He will usually do another sweep cultivation before parsnip tops fill out to suppress new weed growth. He pursues the later escaped weeds as time permits—even after the point that they could lower production—because of their economic impact if they plug his root crop harvester.

Two treatments with the baskets is often all he needs to manage weeds in lettuce. The crop has a short window, usually about 60 days from transplanting to harvest. Ideally, the lettuce field is disked immediately after harvest to prevent weeds from going to seed. Consistent, timely post-harvest cultivation is one of his greatest opportunities for improving whole-farm weed management, Harlow believes. He recognizes a second weed-seed reduction strategy would be more intensive composting of the cattle manure he applies each fall.

He reserves his **in-row finger weeder** (Buddingh Model C) for firm-rooted plants. Flexible rubber fingers 4 inches long radiating from a metal hub scuffle the soil surface right in the row, uprooting small weeds but moving around crops. The tool depends on the resistance of well-established crop plants to work when fingers are set to virtually overlap for total in-row weeding.

Harlow limits the tool to early plantings of corn (spike stage) and well-rooted cole crop transplants such as collards. Shallow-rooted crops—such as lettuce—can't stand to be fingered even if they are well-developed, he's found. And later corn could suffer damage to side roots close to the surface. To determine whether a transplant is ready for finger weeding, he employs the "yank test" rather than count days in the soil. "If it can stay in the soil when I give it a certain tug," he's found, "the weeder won't bother it."

Where crop stalks are large enough to tolerate soil flowing against them, Harlow likes to use his Lilliston **rolling cultivator.** He leaves the spider gangs on his two-row model at the same angle to the row for both early and late passes. Speed makes the difference. He goes through first at 2.5 to 3 mph, doing his best to throw about 1.5 inches of soil at the base of 2-inch corn plants. ("In reality, some don't get anything and others get buried. You have to watch.") About 10 days to two weeks later, a trip through at 5 mph throws up 8-inch hills to smother all weeds and anchor the plants against wind lodging and picking stress. Earlier plantings of corn develop more slowly, and usually require more frequent cultivations than do later, more competitive plantings.

The rolling cultivator works well for first cultivation in potatoes to begin the hilling process, and for collard greens if they jump off to a strong start. In '96, he did no hand weeding on the robust leaf crop until first harvest, thanks to timely cultivation and quick canopy development. Workers hand-pulled mature weeds and weeds that interfered with the five pickings of tender leaves as the crop matured.

To manage the areas between his widely spaced rows of squash, Harlow uses his field cultivator whenever weeds get to be 1 inch tall. He removes the center shanks so he can straddle the crop rows. When he can no longer drive over the bushy plants, he makes a hand-hoeing pass to remove weed pests and thin the crop. Just before the runners extend to close the row middles, he tills the area with a final broadcast pass of the (fully tooled) field cultivator.

His "rescue unit" is a tractor-powered **rotary tiller.** It's his tool of choice to finely incorporate crop residue after harvest, and sometimes is called upon to knock down part of a crop field where weeds have the upper hand—before they go to seed and threaten future crops, as well.

Harlow is convinced that mechanical weeding is the most effective, cost-efficient way to keep crops clean for his system. If he weren't farming organically, he'd keep his same tools and most of the same crops. He says he'd let someone else grow the parsnips and carrots. ■

Intensive controls keep California beds clean

Paul Muller
Full Belly Farm, Guinda, California

- *40 acres vegetables* • *clean tillage* • *sandy clay-loam soils*
- *soil compaction tendency high* • *certified organic* • *18 to 30 inches annual precipitation* • *irrigated 60-inch beds* • *fresh market, wholesale and retail*
- *sweet corn, vine crops, tomatoes, beans, broccoli, lettuces, greens, onions, garlic*

Weed management highlights

Strategies: crop rotation... pre-irrigation and stale seedbed cultivation... flaming... early season mechanical cultivation... cover crops... balanced soil fertility

Tools: precision cultivator, flexible tooling... rolling cultivator... custom toolbar flamer... hand-held flamer... rotary harrow (PTO-powered)... mechanical guidance... offset tractors with belly-mount option

Intensive use of an array of adapted tools has greatly lowered weed pressure over the past 10 years on the Full Belly Farm. Paul Muller handles much of the field and shop work that puts the right steel in the field at the right time. He's brought morning-glory and Johnsongrass under control without herbicides by combining intensive tool use with crop management that improves soil biological health and soil structure, and balances nutrients at optimum levels.

His early season weed control centers on soil preparation, well-timed irrigation and moisture management. Typically, Muller spreads about 8 tons of compost per acre before disking then subsoiling. The compost goes on at an early stage in field preparation or when cover crops are incorporated. He lets cover crop residue decompose for about three weeks after disking before the next tillage pass. That time period varies with moisture, amount of cover residue, how finely the residue is chopped up during incorporation and how thoroughly the residue is incorporated with soil.

Alternatively, Muller has planted corn immediately after thorough incorporation and had good results. "But don't try to plant in between, or the seed is just something else to be composted in the intense biological activity of the soil/residue mix," he says.

His three-row bed shaper uses shanks and shovels to loosen soil so that large V-shaper wings with metal forming panels can throw up soil to make beds 44 inches wide and 8 inches high between 16-inch wide furrows. He's careful to create straight, parallel beds and rows. This makes precision mechanical weed control as easy—and as fast—as possible.

As soon as beds are formed, Muller sprinkle irrigates to stimulate germination of surface weed seeds and breakdown of the cover crop residue. He turns to his weed management tools as soon as weeds emerge and moisture is suitable—certainly before they reach a half inch tall and have consumed precious irrigated moisture.

He lightly tills the beds with a Lely Roterra rotary harrow. (See Chambers, page 69.) He keeps the PTO driven, spinning tines in the top 3 inches of the soil where they dislocate all weeds and leave many on the surface. Muller favors the tool over a rotary tiller because it's faster and he feels it maintains better soil structure in his fields. He reports the Roterra also preserves moisture by creating a loose soil mulch, and its forming shovels re-shape beds nicely.

He turns dry conditions to his advantage by "planting to moisture" all his direct-seeded crops. By pushing back dry soil and creating a row furrow, he places crops into a deeper moisture layer. They thrive while weed seeds have to wait for the next precipitation to germinate. (This is a version of the "lister planting" popularized in the Great Plains.) The practice works about 90 percent of the time, Muller reports, allowing for the once-in-a-decade spring rain that puts moisture everywhere at the wrong time. Metal guidance wheels hug the sides of the bed to firmly align his toolbar-mounted planter.

A V-shaped row opener creates a firmed soil layer at its point that aligns seeds, draws moisture to them from below through capillary action and provides the ideal location for the seed radicle to penetrate lower for more moisture. Disk openers don't provide him these moisture benefits. Small-seeded crops such as lettuce, brassicas and carrots germinate uniformly and ahead of many weeds thanks to this strategy, Muller reports.

"It's always worth the extra wait to pre-irrigate then clean cultivate," he says. "It may delay planting by a week, but it saves dollars on weeding."

For slow-growing crops such as carrots, Muller stymies weed competition with a custom **toolbar flamer.** He attaches three self-vaporizing burners (rated at 350,000 to 750,000 BTUs per hour), centering them 12 inches apart, each one over a three row band of planted but non-emerged carrots. He controls the regulator and shut-off for the toolbar-mounted LP tank from the tractor seat. Groundspeed is 3 to 5 mph. Properly used in a timely fashion, the flamer controls 80 percent of in-row broadleaf weeds, but has little effect on grasses.

When irrigation or rain causes soil to crust before plants emerge, Muller runs crustbreakers to enable seedlings to develop. These tools are widely used in California to cover whole bed tops preemerge, or to run between rows ahead of weed-control tooling. Crustbreakers come in many styles but are commonly made of light angle iron pieces welded into rolling baskets. Preemerge, they run ahead of top knives, which are finely sharpened pieces of straight beveled blade stock about 4 inches wide. The knives may be 6 inches to 5 feet wide and run perpendicular to the bed. Attached to toolbars by straight shanks, they run quite shallow and almost flat, with a slight rise that lets soil easily flow up and over their top surfaces. They can be fashioned in farm shops from road grader steel, with a little grinder work to set a sharp edge.

Muller employs a single-burner, **wand-type hand flamer** for spot weeding when it's too wet for the tractor to do toolbar flaming. He uses a Red Devil burner on a 4-foot pipe. A 5-gallon LP cylinder mounted on a hard-frame backpack fuels the system. He can cover 1 to 2 acres per hour, depending on weed pressure.

Crops jump ahead of weeds when the pre-plant tillage, flaming and dry surface soil steps combine as intended. "When this system works, all weed management tasks go easier for the entire season," Muller finds. One indicator of his consistent early-season success is the limited demand for hand-weeding beyond what's done during hand-thinning: "Half of the time we don't even need it."

For emerging crops, he outfits a 15-foot toolbar with five tool-mounting crossbars. Holding the Alloway vegetable cultivator in place are the same bed-hugging guidance wheels he used on the planter. For each row unit, he clamps on a pair of 12-inch **cutaway disks** that run 0.5 inches to 4 inches from the row; flat, low-profile **vegetable knives** that slice weeds but do not throw much soil; and **tent shields** over the rows that protect tender plants from moving soil.

To cultivate the outside edges of the bed, he uses a pair of curved banana knives per side.

One runs deep, one shallow. Shovels with strong vertical soil-thrusting action clean out the furrow and re-shape the beds. Basket rollers on the back of the unit lightly pack the soil on bed tops to curb moisture loss.

At first pass, when the disks are set only 2 inches apart straddling the rows, he travels 1.5 to 2 mph. At second cultivation he pulls the disks further apart to accommodate crop growth and runs 3 to 4 mph. To save the time involved in re-tooling then readjusting a cultivator toolbar between crops, Muller has a selection of five cultivator toolbars outfitted for different planting arrangements: precision units for single rows or three rows on beds; Lilliston implements for 30-inch rows and single bedded rows; and one to combine cultivating and listing, the making of furrows that precede bed shaping. Minor adjustment as crops develop take relatively little time once row-width and depth settings are fixed.

"If you keep only one tool at a time active, you tend to rob pieces from here and there," he found. "Then you end up looking for those parts when you should be out in the field. With five toolbars ready to go when conditions are just right, our operations are much more timely. Things just work a lot better."

He uses a Lilliston **rolling cultivator** on sweet corn once it reaches 3 inches tall. He sets the five-wheel spider gangs parallel to the row at first pass to work soil and destroy weeds. At this setting, the ground driven, curved arms lift and lightly toss soil but do not move it into the row.

At second cultivation, corn stalks are sturdy enough to tolerate some soil flowing against them to smother in-row weeds. Traveling at about 5 mph, he adjusts the horizontal angle and sideways pitch (allowed by the round mounting standards) to move just the right amount of soil into the row area at the base of the crop plants. (See page 23 for rolling cultivator illustration.)

Because of its several areas of adjustment, setting up a rolling cultivator is especially important to its effective operation. It takes time and experience to learn the skill, but when done well results in excellent control for many users with free-flowing soils. "Once I'm set up, I don't have a problem," says Muller, who encounters virtually no rocks or residue in his fields.

He uses it on other upright crops such as cauliflower, garlic and onions and Romanesco broccoli, all of which he plants in 30-inch rows. He finds that this unusually wide spacing for onions and garlic is justified with the rolling cultivator. He can run it quickly through the rows several times per season, taking out weeds between the rows and smothering in-row weeds, as well.

"This outfit works really well," Muller says. "Many commercial conventional growers use them, and they could get along without herbicides if they wanted to. They use cultivation as insurance, when it could be their main protection."

He believes mechanical weed control will continue to grow in popularity as farmers learn more about organic cropping systems and new crop/tool systems develop. He's glad to be in a place with an abundance of available appropriate technology.

"I live in an area with lots of good tools around that you can buy cheaply," he says. "If you make the effort, you can learn how these tools worked in an era when people knew how to use them." ∎

III. DRYLAND CROPS

The Tools

Cornbelt farmers can expect adequate rainfall in most years. They cultivate in ways that minimize the risk of erosion when the expected precipitation comes.

Dryland farmers just grin when asked about excess precipitation at planting-time. "Usually not a problem 'round here," they say. Some have to leave their fields unplanted for a year (fallowed) just to build up soil moisture. They evaluate every weeding event for its moisture impact.

Weed control implements have been used traditionally to manage the fallow season, the months when volunteer vegetation is managed to reduce moisture withdrawal from fields. "Clean fallow"—keeping soil weed-free—is tillage-intensive, leaves little residue on the soil surface and makes soils vulnerable to wind and water erosion. Residue management tools that reduce that threat grew from Charles Noble's observation in the 1930s that Alberta prairie pastures held top soil while clean fallowed fields were losing it. He introduced undercutting blades up to 12 feet wide for working vast prairies. The sharp V-blades slice through weed roots and lightly disturb the soil surface without burying the above-ground portion. Residue is virtually undiminished.

"Stubble-mulch" implements include a range of lighter-framed tools also designed to undercut weeds and maintain surface residue. These include implements with smaller V-blades, as well as C-shank units with wide sweeps. Chisel plows and field cultivators with increased vertical and fore-to-aft clearance and wide, flat sweeps are also now widely used to manage fallow fields.

Rod weeders were developed to work in loose and low-residue soils. A rotating rod pulls up weeds. Now most units have soil-loosening field cultivator shanks ahead of the rod to aid in weeding and extend the rod weeder's use to higher residue fields. Rod weeders also serve a moisture-managing role during fallow and just prior to planting, as well as a weed-control role in the postplant, preemergence window.

Less familiar is postemergence use of flex-tine weeders, rotary hoes, spike-tooth harrows and skew treaders in young standing grain or dryland row crops. (See "Hoes and harrows to the rescue," page 17.) Skew treaders resemble rotary hoes, but skew arms are straight and there are fewer arms radiating from the wheel hub.

Like other broadcast postemergence cultivation, success depends on timing, using the right tool wisely and relative depths. Tools that scratch the surface need to have ground-engaging parts that have enough muscle to kill shallow-rooted weeds but be elegant enough not to shear off young crop plants. The parts must penetrate deeply enough to get the weeds but not so deep as to damage crop roots. Weeds usually emerge following rainfall, thus timing is complicated by the usual tension: the need for soil dry enough to avoid compaction during the time when weeds are still small enough to control.

Managing weeds in some regions in the mid-'90s was complicated by drought, weed shifts due to no-till herbicide-fallow and invasions of new weeds. Farmers are exploring new tools, new uses of old tools, new crops, new crop sequences and new mixes of tillage, herbicide and cultural options.

Field cultivator (sweeps)

Overview: Shanks and sweeps much like those used on row-crop cultivators. Shanks stagger-spaced on four or five toolbars to do broadcast tillage 2" to 5" deep across the full tool width. Field cultivators are widely used in mulch-tillage of relatively light residue, low herbicide systems to control successive flushes of weeds prior to planting. Wide, low-profile sweeps (6" to 12" on C-shanks, 3" to 11" on S-tines) optimize weed control and minimize soil mixing. Also used widely for secondary preplant tillage. Leaves 50 to 75 percent residue; impact varies with speed and sweep design.

Design features: Shanks fasten directly to a toolbar without the parallel linkage of row-crop cultivators. Spring cushioned or spring-trip auto-reset shanks recommended for soils with underground obstructions. Net spacing (of all shanks on all toolbars) is 4" to 7" for S-tines, 6" to 9" for C-shanks.

The high number of shanks disturbs residue and opens the soil surface to drying more than other shanked, dryland implements. Some C-shanks are "edge-bent" (formed so that the narrow dimension of the shank faces forward on the bottom half of the shank) for greater strength and stability with less soil impact and horsepower drag. C-shank stock for field cultivators ranges from 0.5" to 0.88" thick and 1.75" to 2" wide.

Vertical clearance is 20" to 27", sweep tip to bottom of toolbar. Spike-tooth or straight flex-tine harrow attachments often added to level soil, control weeds and incorporate chemicals.

Integral (3-point hitch) models maximum 25' wide; drawn type for wider versions.

▶ **Model for comparison:** 22' folding frame, drawn/pull type
  Rec. PTO HP: 125   **Speed:** 4 to 7 mph   **Avg. list price:** $9,780*
  *Excluding $21,600 unit with standard floating hitch, high-cushion trip and thicker shanks.

Width range (all makers/all models): 12' to 62'

Sources: 15, 26, 47, 54, 71, 78, 79, 93   **Farmers:** Fernholz, Harlow, Jacobson

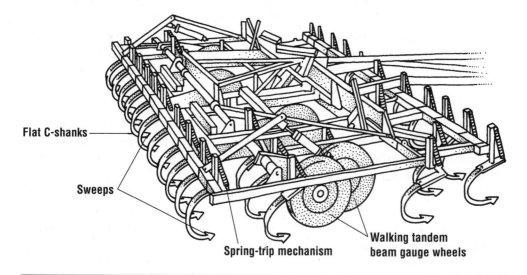

Flat C-shanks

Sweeps

Spring-trip mechanism

Walking tandem beam gauge wheels

Chisel plow (with sweeps)

0"	2"	4"	6"	8"	10"	12"	18"	24"	30"	36"

WEED height range (annuals) estimate

■ suitable   ▨ less suitable   ☐ unsuitable

Weed control varies with soil conditions and weed density.

Overview: Heavier construction and fewer shanks improve residue management function compared with a field cultivator; used under a wider range of conditions, leaving soil rougher. Can be operated deep enough to shatter hardpans and improve water infiltration. For weed control in untilled soil, sweeps 12" to 18" wide do an effective job. When operated 4" to 6" deep at moderate speeds with low profile sweeps, can preserve 80 percent of residue.

Design features: Chisel plow shanks are usually 12" apart. Optional 16" spacing for better residue handling. Some C-shanks are "edge-bent" (formed so that the narrow dimension of the shank faces forward on the bottom half of the shank) for greater strength and stability with less soil impact and horsepower drag. C-shank stock for chisel plows is nearly always 1.25" thick and 2" wide, giving shanks more rigidity and less vibration than field cultivator shanks. Vertical clearance 27" to 32"; fore-to-aft clearance of 30" to 40" between toolbars.

▶ **Model for comparison:** 23' folding frame, drawn/pull type, spring-reset shanks
   Rec. PTO HP: 150 to 210   **Speed:** 5 mph   **List price:** $12,755

Width range (all makers/all models): 11' to 53'

Sources: 15, 26, 47, 54, 71, 81, 93   **Farmers:** Artho, Cavin, Jacobson, McKaskle, Reeder, Smith

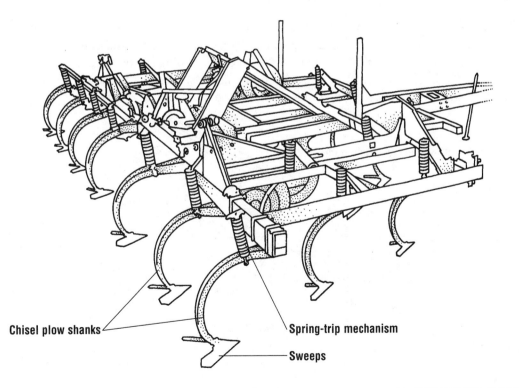

Chisel plow shanks — Spring-trip mechanism — Sweeps

Stubble mulch blade plow

(2' to 4' V-blades; 26" sweeps)

WEED height range (annuals) estimate

█ suitable   ▓ less suitable   ☐ unsuitable

Weed control varies with soil conditions and weed density.

Overview: Intermediate types of tools that combine tillage aspect of chisel plows with residue-maintaining aspects of the heavier wide-blade sweep plow. Used for first tillage after crop harvest where a depth of 3" to 6" is sufficient. Limits moisture loss better compared with chisel plow by conserving more residue due to fewer soil openings from more widely spaced shanks. Cannot provide rough soil surface to control wind erosion and trap moisture that a chisel plow with shovels can. Saves 75 to 95 percent of surface residue.

Design features: Some tools in this broad category use single-piece V-blades that fit on V-shaped base standards (as illustrated). These bases usually operate deeper than do tools using 26" low-profile sweeps. V-blades 36" to 48" wide mount on straight shanks 34" to 44" on center. The flat "wheatland" type sweeps mount on elongated chisel-plow type shanks 20" on center. Best results in high residue with two ranks; some units have three ranks. Fore-to-aft clearance 24" to 40" between ranks—more distance lets more residue flow through.

▶ **Model for Comparison:** 24' folding frame, drawn/pull type, with coulters (not illustrated)
Rec. PTO HP: 160 to 200   **Speed:** 5 mph   **List price:** $17,000

Width range (all makers/all models): 18' to 63'

Sources: 9, 79, 81, 93   **Farmers:** Artho, Berning, Cavin

Note: Rolling mulch treaders are optional rear attachments widely used on residue management units. Treaders feature curved flat teeth radiating with a slight twist to an 18.5" diameter from a central hub. The teeth ends pin residue into the tilled soil (to prevent blowing and hasten decomposition) and increase weed kill at the soil surface. Because of their aggressive action, treaders must be used with caution or removed when preserving residue is more important than working it in.

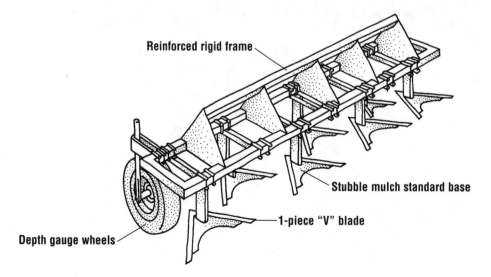

Reinforced rigid frame

Stubble mulch standard base

1-piece "V" blade

Depth gauge wheels

Wide blade sweep plow
(5' to 7' V-blades)

Overview: Often generically called "Noble blades" due to the Canadian manufacturer, these implements are perhaps the ultimate steel force for weed management. Reinforced, box-beam frames support a single V-shaped blade per section. Overlapping blades 5' to 12' wide run 3" to 6" below the surface to cut off roots of any tall plant, while leaving the weed stems and crop firmly embedded at the surface. The implement can leave 85 to 95 percent residue on the surface if operated at least 3" deep.

The blades will kill any tap root but may not disturb shallow-rooted weeds. Pull-behind mulch treaders will uproot these little weeds. Recommended use is at a depth 0.5" to 1.0" above the moisture line, so that weeds will have no moisture to revive them after being severed. Adjustment is critical, but often left unchecked. The blades must be level side to side, and turnbuckles must be set to relieve any pressure between frame-lift cylinders.

Hard-surfaced blades self-sharpen, increasing weed kill and operating depth consistency while decreasing draft. Avoid running repeatedly at the same depth to reduce plowpan tendency.

Design features: The V-base is constructed of angle iron with its angled edge facing upward. The V-blade is bolted to the leading edge, its arms only slightly sweeping back on each side so that the blade wings run at nearly a right angle to the direction of travel. Welded steel plates create rigid upright standards. Shear bolts or hydraulic cushioning protect against obstructions.

▶ **Model for comparison:** 31' folding frame, 5' blades (no mulch treaders)
   Rec. PTO HP: 150   **Speed:** 5 to 6 mph   **List price avg:** $20,000

Width range (all makers/all models): 14.3' to 66.5'

Sources: 73, 93   **Farmers:** Berning, Jacobson, Reeder

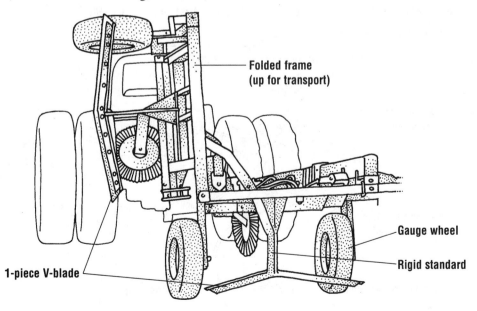

Folded frame
(up for transport)

Gauge wheel

Rigid standard

1-piece V-blade

Rod weeder

0"	2"	4"	6"	8"	10"	12"	18"	24"	30"	36"

WEED height range (annuals) estimate

■ suitable   ▨ less suitable   □ unsuitable

Weed control varies with soil conditions and weed density.

Overview: Rotating subsurface rod action pulls and uproots weeds, depositing them on the surface fully exposed to sun and wind. Under heavy weed conditions, the net effect can be a weed residue mulch. The rod leaves a layer of loose soil as its main mulching effect that deters weed regrowth and lessens subsoil moisture evaporation. Another benefit is the rod's slightly compacting effect on soil at its lower edge. "Setting the moisture line" stops capillary action and seals moisture in suitable soil types. This combination of benefits is ideal for minimizing weeding passes while maintaining residue.

Rigid or flex frame rod weeders work in listed (furrowed) row-crop fields in final seedbed preparation, and to weed *after* planting where germinating crop seeds are deep enough for the rod to pass over them. The pass firms seed into moisture and gives it a weed-free, mulched covering to jump ahead of later weeds. If the seedbed benefits aren't needed, stubble-mulch tools may be preferable to rod weeders. They can leave about as much residue but have no moving parts to maintain.

Design features: The leading edge of the rod spins upward as it travels 1.5" to 2.5" below the surface. Rods can be round, square or hexagonal of 0.78" to 1.12" high-carbon steel stock. They are fastened by U-shaped ground arms to a toolbar. Rods are powered by a reversing chain drive on ground-driven systems, hydraulics, or PTO. Most rod weeder implements have field cultivator sweeps running ahead of the rod to loosen the soil profile. This helps to maintain consistent rod depth.

Section lengths (7', 10' or 12') overlap. Springs or hydraulics return rod sections to the soil after they trip up (10" to 20") to clear obstructions.

Some makers provide rod weeder attachments for field cultivators, chisel plows or residue-managing plows. The rods add weeding, leveling and mulching effects and set a moisture line.

▶ **Model for comparison:** 36' ground driven, pull/drawn type, with sweeps
  Rec. PTO HP: 100 to 150   **Speed:** 5 to 7 mph   **List price:** $13,190

Width range (all makers/all models): 28' to 64'

Sources: 22, 57, 71, 79, 81   **Farmers:** Cavin, Smith

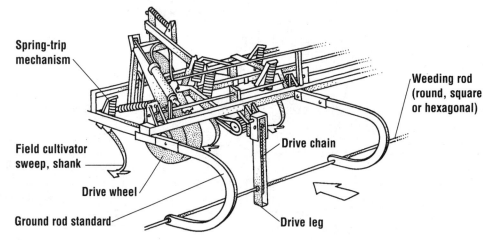

- Spring-trip mechanism
- Weeding rod (round, square or hexagonal)
- Field cultivator sweep, shank
- Drive chain
- Drive wheel
- Ground rod standard
- Drive leg

Tandem disk harrow

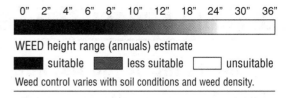

WEED height range (annuals) estimate

■ suitable   ▨ less suitable   ☐ unsuitable

Weed control varies with soil conditions and weed density.

Overview: The cutting and mixing action of a disk harrow varies with the diameter, weight and concavity of its blades; blade spacing; the angle of the disk harrow gang relative to the direction of travel; and operating speed. In dryland farming, the disk harrow can help prepare over-wintered stubble or fallowed land for seeding.

In a mulch-till system that includes soil-structure improvement as part of its weed management, a tandem disk with 22" diameter blades on 9" spacing could create a fall seedbed for a winter cover crop by partially incorporating corn stubble; knock down the cover crop in spring; create a rough seedbed of overwintered residue for residue-managing planters; or run shallowly just before planting to kill all surface weeds. Larger diameter blades, or blades that are spaced farther apart, run at a higher speed, or set at angles of more than 18 percent are more aggressive.

Design features: Tandem disks gangs are configured like a bowtie: the front gangs, left and right, lead with the outside ends ahead and angle back toward the center; the back gangs, in the mirror position, have the inner ends leading in the center of the tool and outside ends angling back. Gang angle is fixed at 18 or 20 degrees, or adjustable at lesser angles.

Offset disk harrow frames have two straight gangs, one behind the other, on a strong central H-frame. The gangs angle in opposite directions. Gang angle is adjustable, usually in the range of 25 to 48 percent. Offset disks, outfitted with heavier blades up to 28" diameter, are used more often for primary tillage and high residue.

▶ **Model for comparison:** 21' tandem pull/drawn type
  Rec. PTO HP: 120 to 170   **Speed:** 4 to 8 mph   **List price:** $17,240

Width range (all makers/all models): 6' to 23' for offset; 6' to 33' for tandem.

Sources: 26, 47, 54, 93, 95, 104

Farmers: Bennett, de Wilde, Erisman, Gemme, Harlow, Kenagy, McKaskle, Spray, Muller

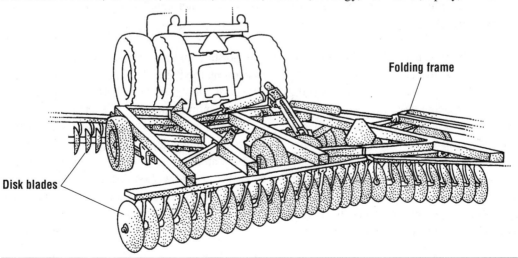

Folding frame

Disk blades

Dryland Crops: The Farmers

Tillage in the Texas Panhandle:
Matching wits with clay, wind and drought

Dale Artho
Wildorado, Texas
• *3,600 acres* • *Grain sorghum, wheat, fallow (in thirds)*
• *Clay loam soils* • *Half of acreage receives supplemental furrow irrigation* • *17-19 inches annual rainfall* • *sporadic, intense thundershowers* • *stocker cattle on winter-grazed wheat*

Weed management highlights

Strategies: inter-row cultivation... winter wheat grazing... fallow mulch tillage... limited herbicides (spot-spray, burndown and banded pre-emerge)... narrow rows for quick canopy... staggered planting dates to keep weed-control needs within labor/machine capacity... summer-annual forage crop

Tools: cultivators with knives, sweeps and furrow openers... mechanical guidance... chisel plow with wide sweeps... fallow-managing tool with wide sweeps

Farming on the High Plains of the Texas pan-handle is about true grit, about taking on odds that farmers elsewhere would call gambling.

Dale Artho's clay loam soil can harden like concrete, or crust to shed water that crops need to survive the baking summer sun. Summer rains come in torrents—when they come at all. Virtually any cropping choice can be right, or wrong, depending on the wind or the rain or the markets.

"You just hope you do the right thing at least 50 percent of the time," says Artho. He uses high-residue cultivators, conservation tillage and crop spacing to whittle down his use of herbicides. He's gone to mulch tillage and 240-foot-wide crop strips to check wind erosion. Anything else that cuts risk, saves moisture or boosts yields on his mile-square sections of land is a welcome addition.

Much like vegetable growers in sunny California, High Plains farmers can depend on a rain-free, early summer planting season 9 years out of 10. Artho plants sorghum with a 10-inch herbicide band over the row. He plants two rows, 30 inches apart, on 60-inch-wide beds that are 5 inches high. Each row is 15 inches in from a side. Dry weather usually keeps inter-row weed pressure low early in the season but also inhibits herbicide action.

To help sorghum germination, he designs all tillage passes throughout the year to maximize soil moisture for this early summer season. No-till systems he tried often left his soil too unmanageable during this period and led to weed problems.

To minimize the risk of encountering more weed pressure than his steel could handle, Artho limits how many acres of sorghum will need to be cultivated at one time. He staggers planting times for several weeks starting in late April (on irrigated fields) through late June (dryland) to facilitate timely weed control.

"When this plan works, I've got a great window to cultivate," he explains. He has two cultivators—one 16-row and one eight-row—for the 1,200 acres of sorghum he plants each year, so he needs to stretch out the weeding time period.

He built the larger cultivator, starting with a 40-foot, 5x7-inch folding toolbar. He added 20-inch **flat sweeps** on 1.25x3-inch straight shanks, stabilizer coulters and metal **guide cones** to run in the furrows left at planting. His cultivation trigger is the arrival of witchgrass—also called Colorado grass or ticklegrass (*Panicum capillare* L.). "It comes up, explodes in growth and sucks water from the soil at a staggering rate," Artho says. "In a single day a field can go from being too wet to being too dry. And the grass has to be controlled, or it will cripple production."

Other weedy invaders in the sorghum are pigweed (Palmer amaranth), kochia and bindweed. He can cultivate with sweeps or use herbicide, adding either option to other required tillage at no extra tractor cost—but herbicide would be an added expense.

One job is to improve water retention between the two rows of sorghum on each bed. His Roll-A-Cone diker intermittently drags then releases paddles of its large spider wheel to create mini-reservoirs. Trapping water in the gallon-sized depressions gives it more time to soak into the subsoil. Artho's 40-percent-clay loam soil can hold up to 10 inches of precipitation and accept it at 6 inches per hour when the soil surface is open. But that infiltration rate plummets to almost nothing if soil is crusted on top.

The paddle assemblies are attached to a secondary toolbar attached to his cultivator. The depressions prevent rainfall from running off his field and give the soil time to absorb the water. He usually makes this pass when sorghum is 8 to 10 inches tall.

Performing the three-fold tillage operation is his highly valued Hitchcock **high residue cultivator.** The rugged eight-row precision tool was designed for sugarbeet production, one of Artho's former crops. That heritage makes it well-suited to cultivate the flat bed tops and furrows between the beds.

The cultivator's gangs include 20-inch smooth **coulters** to cut residue; gauge wheels to keep tools gliding at an even depth through the soil; **cutaway disks** that peel residue and weed seeds away from the rows; thin side-knives (**vegetable knives**), right-angle types for the flat surfaces and curved types to handle the bed sides; 20-inch, **low-profile sweeps** to undercut weeds on both sides of the rows; furrow-opener **ridging wings** (mounted just above the sweeps) to throw soil into the rows for the hilling effect; and more furrow shovels to reshape the furrows between the beds.

The diker creates the mini-reservoirs down the middle of each bed. The pass leaves each sorghum row between two water sources—a furrow for supplemental irrigation and the line of reservoirs to capture any rain through the season. Artho usually supplies water about 35 days after planting when the potential number of seeds per head is being determined. Moisture stress at this time cripples yield.

Holding the cultivator tightly in alignment with the crop rows are thin **metal guidance wheels** and guide sleds that run against the 5-inch high sides of the raised beds. "This was Hitchcock's 'pre-electronic' guidance system, and it still works fine," says Artho.

Artho raises forage wheat for his stocker cattle and grain wheat for harvest. Both types of fields will need ticklegrass control by August. He leaves all the stubble on the surface to prevent wind erosion and to build soil organic matter. Recently, however, he's had little biomass to work with. In '94, '95 and '96, drought kept stubble under 6 inches tall on some of his farms, while late spring freezes or hail arrested stalks at 12 to 18 inches on others. He explains that in a "good year," the area's dryland wheat yields 30 bushels per acre.

He uses a Quinstar Fallowmaster™ for the August field pass. It has two ranks of chisel-plow shanks mounted on a braced frame. The tool is structurally stronger than a field cultivator but is lighter than a blade plow. It pulls staggered 26-inch sweeps spaced 20 inches apart.

The pass kills weeds, leaves residue to trap snow, and opens up the soil surface to let water infiltrate. Afterward, there's enough residue left (70 to 85 percent in a good year) to minimize moisture loss. If rains sprout more weeds, Artho uses herbicide to maintain the residue cover.

In spring he runs the Fallowmaster™ again. He hitches a tank caddy on to spot-spray bindweed (*Convolvulus arvensis* L., called morning-glory in some regions).

Artho finds technique is important in this combination pass. A postemergent herbicide works best where the weed is undisturbed and not covered with soil particles. When he approaches a patch of weeds, he slows down, turns on wide-angle nozzles and raises the sweeps out of the soil—all *before* he reaches the target weeds. Once he's past the patch, he drops the sweeps then turns off the sprayer.

The care with which Artho interweaves tillage and herbicides in this maneuver symbolizes his overall approach to weed control. "I'm controlling weeds with tools to manage moisture, and I use economical chemicals when I have to," he muses. "It's a blend that works in my predictably unpredictable, extreme conditions." ■

Beds and rod weeder boost diverse crops on Kansas farm

Jerome Berning
Marienthal, Kansas

• *1,800 acres (600 of them fallow)* • *flat fields, silt loam soil*
• *seasonal deep-well furrow irrigation* • *half of acreage is organic*
• *weeds: kochia, pigweed, velvetleaf* • *16 inches precipitation;*
rapid evaporation • *row crops in 30-inch rows on 60-inch beds*
• *wheat (hard red winter), yellow corn, blue corn, soybeans, sunflowers,*
speciality seeds

Weed management highlights

Strategies: crop rotation... fallow cultivation... mechanical controls... herbicides

Tools: rotary hoe... cultivator... rod weeder... sweep plow... stubble mulch plow... rotary tiller

More steel means fewer headaches for Jerome Berning. Recent additions give him better control in maintaining 600 acres of fallow land and in managing early season weeds in tilled, bedded (furrowed) soil.

Berning, who farms half his acres under herbicide-free organic management, keeps his systems as flexible as he can to stay in synch with moisture, soil condition and weed pressure. He uses four rotation sequences: wheat soybeans-corn-fallow (organic); wheat-fallow-wheat (organic and conventional); corn-fallow-corn (organic); and wheat-soybean-corn (conventional).

Relatively dry, cool spring conditions allow Berning's annual crops to germinate with or ahead of the first major flush of weeds. Some farmers find late planting gives them a chance to cultivate early weeds before planting crops into warmer soil for robust germination. But

Berning's experience is that early planting works best for him.

Those planting dates let crops catch what passes for the "rainy season" in dry western Kansas—a time when he can expect a number of half-inch or quarter-inch rains. Careful preplant tillage creates smooth beds 60 inches wide and removes early weeds in the top inch or so of soil.

His spring tillage for annual crops includes several steps.

Bed preparation. After chopping then disking corn or sunflower stubble, Berning forms beds by making furrows about 1 foot deep and 1 foot wide every 60 inches with "lister" shovels. These shovels have flared, stocky, fairly vertical wings to throw soil up and out in both directions.

These furrows nicely divide up the fields, guide the tractor and implement wheels, and later carry irrigation water through the field.

Preplant weeding. Rains are possible during this pre-plant tillage season. But building up soil moisture is critical if annual crops are to start off strong. To assure topsoil moisture, Berning pre-irrigates the unplanted field. He greets the first flush of small, white-root weeds and larger weed survivors with one of two weed tools, depending upon the level of residue and whether its an organic or conventional field.

He goes with his 30-foot Tilrovator **rotary tiller** if he needs to incorporate residue or pre-plant herbicides. The tool works in the top 4 inches of soil with its hard-surfaced, L-shaped blades designed for shallow mixing and cutting action.

But Berning uses a 30-foot **rod weeder** if wiping out the weeds and achieving the finished bed condition are his goals. The tool's PTO-powered, 1-inch square rod turns underground to flip up the weeds and "flow the soil across the beds" for even distribution, Berning reports. The pass at 4 mph knocks down the beds to about 8 inches tall.

"The rod weeder means less row-crop tillage," Berning explains. "Before, I used a disk just before planting to take care of the weeds. Then we had to furrow after we cultivated so we could irrigate. With the rod weeder we can make furrows early, maintain them and conserve moisture."

For the second irrigation and weeding sequence, he runs the weeder faster (7 mph) and shallower (1 to 2 inches deep). This keeps the moisture seal of the previous pass intact and does not stimulate new weed seeds.

Rotary hoeing. After planting corn 1.5 inches deep and soybeans an inch deep a month later, Berning follows quickly with his 30-foot **standard rotary hoe.** Planting times are mid-April for yellow corn, early May for blue corn and mid-May for soybeans. If other crops fail, he can plant sunflowers as late as mid-June. He drives the John Deere 400 hoe 6 to 9 mph as soon as weed seedlings pop through or a rain-induced soil crust threatens to prevent crop emergence.

The hoe's two gauge wheels run in furrows bordering the two outside beds of the six-bed pass. The wheels stabilize the tool to prevent rough spots in the field from causing one side of the hoe to gouge down into the planted crop. Berning estimates that 90 percent of the benefit he derives from the rotary hoe is for weed control, with only 10 percent being for crust-breaking.

Beyond the white-root weeds it's known for controlling, Berning also depends on the hoe to pluck up larger weeds. These are usually plants with a developed root ball that were dislocated by the rod weeder then began regrowing in the soil.

He has no shields on his cultivator to protect plants from moving soil, so Berning runs his rotary hoe in more mature crops than some farmers. He estimates maximum heights at 10 inches for yellow corn and 6 inches for sunflowers. Because blue corn tillers, the stalks will range from 3 to 10 inches at the last hoe pass.

He experiences some plugging of his hoe with corn and sunflower root crowns. He's trying simple flat iron **extender arms** that double the space between front and rear wheels. The expansion to 15 inches allows residue to pass between the hoe wheels more easily.

Cultivation. His 30-foot row-crop cultivator features 18- to 24-inch sweeps on the bed tops between the 30-inch rows, with lister shovels in the furrows. He selects the two types of tooling for opposite results: the one-piece flat sweeps move virtually no soil into the row, while the upturned wings of the listers deflect soil up and to either side, reforming the furrow.

Berning targets pigweed and kochia with his single cultivation. Thanks to dry conditions after the corn reaches 10 to 15 inches tall, weeds aren't much of a problem for the rest of the season. He usually hand-rogues escapes in soybeans, averaging $8 per acre per year for labor.

Post-harvest tillage is left until spring so the stalks can collect snow on the fields over winter. Berning runs his double-rotor, rotary stalk chopper over all the cornfields, then hits the 140- to 180-bushel-per-acre yellow corn fields twice with a disk. The blue corn, which typically yields only 45 to 80 bushels per acre, needs just a single disking.

In his wheat-fallow-wheat system, tillage usually starts in August after the late-June wheat harvest. The first pass is with his 30-foot Flex King **wide-blade sweep plow.** This dryland specialty tool has blade assemblies 6 feet wide on 5-foot centers. Each replaceable V-blade attaches to an angle iron base at the bottom of rigid standards. Hard-surfacing keeps the blades running through Berning's soils for four seasons before they need to be replaced.

The mass of the sweep plow gives it the ability to keep the leading edge of the large blades submerged 3 to 6 inches below the soil surface. The 3.5-inch height of the angle iron base prevents it from working more shallowly without bulldozing soft soil or popping out of harder soil. Berning avoids using the blade plow when soil is moist so as not to cause compaction.

The sweep plow's widely spaced standards cut few surface paths through the residue. As long as it runs at least 4 inches below the surface, it can leave 85 to 95 percent of non-fragile residue on the surface.

If volunteer wheat or other weeds become enough of a threat, Berning makes a second sweep plow pass through the wheat stubble in late fall. During the following year before replanting wheat in mid-September, Berning will make four to six tillage passes to control weeds. Each time his goal is to leave as much residue— and cause as little moisture loss—as possible.

He wants to go shallower in the last several cultivations to bring subsoil moisture closer to the surface. His sweep plow ridges soil during these passes, which causes moisture loss and clod formation in the peaks. It also leaves some well-rooted 6-inch kochia weeds unkilled. The repeated plowing seems to train their dense, fine roots to grow sideways.

"I've got **flex-tine harrow** sections on the sweep plow to help with weeding," says Berning. Mulch treaders would be more aggressive at knocking soil from the kochia weed rootcrowns.

He has that extra-tough weed fighter on his new 42-foot Quinstar Fallow Master II™, a **stubble mulch plow** with 26-inch sweeps on 20-inch centers. Each 7-foot section has a 7-foot angled rolling bar of treader wheels (curved, bevel-tipped arms) on 7-inch centers. Now he has to balance between too much and too little. "The treaders can chew up brittle residue and powder the soil if things are dry. I watch the results carefully toward planting time," he says.

The sweep's flat profile sweeps allows them to travel within 2 inches of the surface without causing ridging, yet retain 80 to 90 percent of non-fragile residue.

Tillage has been crucial to manage the late-summer moisture that comes up from lower soil levels. "With chem-fallow (using herbicides to control weeds), our soil cracks open and the moisture escapes," he says.

Berning credits better tillage equipment with decreasing weed pressure over the 25 years he's been farming. First, higher horsepower tractors on the farm in the '80s let him drop the sweep blade low enough to cut off large weeds. Now the lighter-draft fallow tool lets him finesse the final fallow passes. He's got a better chance now to approach wheat planting with weeds down and moisture up on the west-Kansas prairie. ■

Dry times on the High Plains give advantage to minimal tillage

Jim Cavin
Hereford, Texas
• *2,400 acres • permanent wheel rows • sorghum, wheat (hard red winter), irrigated corn • strip tillage in continuous sorghum*
• *summer fallow to gather moisture • 18 inches annual precipitation*
• *clay and clay-loam soil types*

Weed management highlights

Strategies: minimum tillage... reduced-chemical fallow... cultivation... herbicides (mostly preplant)

Tools: cultivators... rotary hoe... disk-steer guidance system... stubble mulch plow... chisel plow

Jim Cavin tried no-till farming in his 1.5-mile long fields of grain, but finds that mulch tillage works much better in his heavy clay loam soils. And after three consecutive dry years then a stiff cost hike for irrigation-pump natural gas in early 1997, he believes that maintaining residue year-round and managing soil conditions at planting are more critical than ever.

With no-till, he encountered increasing weed problems, despite his use of recommended herbicides. He also was unable to create a favorable seedbed environment during the harsh High Plains springs. "I lost out on this untilled clay loam soil that always seemed to be too hard or too wet or too dry," Cavin recalls. "With mulch tillage, I can scrape together enough loose soil and residue to give the seed moisture, air and a chance to survive."

He combines mechanical weed control with three tillage jobs: fallow management, furrowing of crop beds and "diking" (see page 95).

Continuous dryland grain sorghum is his main crop. Forty-inch rows give plenty of room for residue dispersion. Compared with 30-inch rows, the spacing gives crop roots more soil moisture to scavenge, but lessens the canopy shading effect to suppress weeds.

He plants sorghum deep enough to find moisture. Residue managers—finger wheel attachments ahead of his planter opener—clear residue out of the row area. Cavin bands or broadcasts preplant broadleaf herbicides, depending on weed and residue conditions. Dry surface soil often helps to keep weed pressure low through the early weeks of sorghum growth. Cultivation takes care of grasses that find enough moisture to emerge, but he has to hit large-leafed devil's claw weed with a mix of atrazine and crop oil.

Cavin makes his first weed-control pass with a 40-foot John Deere **standard rotary hoe.** The tool has close-spaced wheels that can plug in high-residue situations. But it works for him in the untilled sorghum residue primarily because of relatively low yields—2,500 pounds per acre on average. That's about as much residue as an Illinois farmer would get from a 45-bushel-per acre corn crop. Further decreasing the residue-tangling potential in the widely spaced rows is a spring-time pass with a rolling stalk chopper.

"I drive the hoe at 10 miles per hour and watch closely for crop and weed impact," says Cavin. "On a good, long day I can hoe 400 acres."

He begins to cultivate as soon as the sorghum plants can tolerate soil flowing against them. He pulls three sweeps between the wide crop rows with his 12-row, **high-residue cultivator.** A 24-inch flat sweep slices down the middle, while two 12-inch low-profile sweeps run to within 4 inches of the row on either side. That provides a 4-inch overlap within the row for extra weed-cutting action. He assembled the rig with Roll-A-Cone components on a Bigham Brothers toolbar setup. Both firms specialize in regional tillage equipment.

"This tool will last for a long time, and I figure I spend about $2.50 an acre for diesel to pull it," says Cavin.

He's had good success with the unit, even when volunteer sorghum, annual grasses and the seeded sorghum have all been 5 to 6 inches tall. If his herbicides don't work, he'll go through a second time.

He budgets one cultivation as a no-cost

operation because of his need to "dike" the fields. Each depression is about 4 feet long and 6 inches deep.

At 4 mph max, it's not a quick field pass. But it's necessary. "We get most of all our rainfall in summer. You have to have these reservoirs, or you lose it," says Cavin.

An Orthman Tracker **disk-steer guidance system** keeps the cultivator aligned with the rows. On first pass, fist-sized bulb weight sensors drag ahead of the cultivator in a furrow made at planting. The sensors can detect a change in orientation between the cultivator toolbar and the furrow. Their movement is picked up in the sensor box, which then triggers automatic adjustments by the rear-mounted disks. He switches to plant-sensing wands on second pass, when stalks are stiff enough to be detected by the wands.

Weed pressure in sorghum is usually light, rarely requiring more than a single cultivation. His sweep cultivator takes out the weeds and volunteer corn. He makes the pass as early as possible to avoid root pruning and to cover as few milo shoots as possible. Cavin tries to maximize the secondary grain heads. In '96, he planted about 32,000 plants per acre but ended up harvesting an estimated 55,000 to 60,000 stalks per acre. Yield was 6,800 pounds per acre, with the plants supporting two or three heads each.

Wheat follows a year of moisture-conserving fallow, a no-crop season that builds up soil moisture for the following season. After fall harvest of corn or sorghum, the field is left untouched throughout the winter. When spring rains stimulate weeds, Cavin controls them using a chisel plow outfitted with 18-inch sweeps on 12-inch centers. He works the soil each time rain causes a new surge of weed germination, usually three or four times per summer. It's been fewer in the recent dry years. He plants wheat about the first week of October.

With no livestock, he derives no grazing

benefit—a common way that other farmers in the area get double use from wheat fields. But the earlier-planted grazing wheat also takes more moisture. "Wheat should help hold snow, but we've not been having enough moisture to get the wheat tall enough to stop much snow, and we've not been having much snow to be caught."

He controls weeds at first tillage after wheat harvest with a **stubble mulch plow.** It has straight shanks on 40-inch centers with 42-inch flat blades. The replaceable V-blades attach in a way similar to the much larger wide-blade sweep plow. Cavin made the 40-foot-wide tool himself and pulls it with a 200 HP tractor. Running depth is 2 to 3 inches at about 5 mph.

He makes succeeding fallow passes with a chisel plow equipped with 18-inch sweeps on 12-inch centers. Cavin uses this tool only for weed control and feels it causes less compaction than the much heavier wide-blade sweep plow. He uses the chisel plow as soon as the soil dries enough to avoid compaction but before the soil becomes too hard and weeds become too large.

He leaves his corn stalks untilled and unchopped over winter to hold soil in place and to minimize residue loss from tilling. "I have to have standing stalks to stop the blowing snow of February and March," Cavin explains. "Otherwise, it just keeps on going."

He's been managing residue more carefully for several years to depend less on irrigation water. It now appears he started early on a path others will need to walk, too. When moisture was relatively abundant, clean tillage of weeds worked because there was more groundwater available and farmers could afford to pump it.

Three years of drought—when the area received only about half the 18 inches per year it used to get—continues to draw down underground water supplies. Then in early '97 he received notice that the price of the natural gas that runs the pumps was increasing 44 percent.

These conditions confirm his determination to find effective, low-cost dryland strategies.

Judging subsoil moisture adequacy at planting time is a critical part of dryland farming. Cavin is developing his diagnostic skills using a steel probe to detect when there's enough soil moisture to raise corn in his non-irrigated fields. This "penetrometer" is a carbon steel bar with a small round ball on the bottom. If he can push it down 5 to 6 feet, he knows he's got enough moisture for corn, which is less drought-tolerant than grain sorghum. Rains during the season have to provide the rest of the moisture.

Weed pressure in corn comes from kochia, a tough weed that herbicides won't control beyond an inadequate 75 percent. Cavin plows before planting to bury the weed seeds. He's using some new corn seed from lines that are resistant to grass herbicides. He looks to these chemicals for control of johnsongrass and sandbur grass.

Another way to make better use of water is to use a single irrigation system on two crops on different furrowed fields. This limits water use and spreads out the cultivation window to prevent the usual early summer weed pressure overlap.

"In '96 I planted 100-day corn on April first and had it in black layer on the first of August," Cavin says. Yield was about 200 bushels per acre. "Then I shut that pump down and diverted the water to a late sorghum field that I planted in June. The crop was just at the fill stage where moisture will improve the yield."

Some farmers in the region rely on extensive herbicide applications with just one pass of a sweep plow, or extensive tillage with repeated disking, subsoiling and field cultivators. Some still burn their field residue. "Change comes slow here," Cavin acknowledges, but drier conditions call for innovations. He's convinced he'll make money over the long haul by learning new ways to manage residue with mulch tillage and limited herbicides. ∎

Long rotations, tall crops, right steel suppress northern Dakota weeds

Terry Jacobson
Wales, North Dakota
- *640 acres, flat fields • organic grains and livestock*
- *glacial till, clay loam soils • 5 to 6 percent soil organic matter*
- *one of shortest growing seasons in continental U.S.*
- *18 inches precipitation • crops: spring wheat, barley, oats, flax, sweetclover, rye, sunflowers, alfalfa.*

Weed management highlights

Strategies: crop rotation... tall varieties... delayed planting... pre-plant weeding... mechanical cultivation... soil structure management... fallow tillage residue management

Tools: rod weeder at planting... stiff-tine drag harrow... field cultivator... row-crop cultivator... chisel plow... wide sweep plow

Wild mustard loves the cool springs of northern North Dakota. It comes on strong just when annual crops are getting started.

Innovative farmers elsewhere could use winter grains to suppress the early invaders, but it's too cold here for milling grains to survive. Lots of other operators would use a non-selective herbicide to get a clean start, but organic farmer Terry Jacobson has long ago forsaken that option.

Instead he weaves together a flexible rotation of tall grain varieties, underseeded cover crops, carefully applied tillage, and delayed crop planting to thwart weeds.

The givens of his crop rotation sequence are wheat (Year 1 and Year 4) and disked-down yellow blossom sweet clover (Year 3 and Year 6). These rotate through the sequence that stretches to six years to keep confectionery sunflowers (Year 5) from appearing on the same soil any more often.

The other two slots are flex years for short-season annuals that allow him to respond to market opportunities. Year 2 is open for oats or flax. Year 5 can be sunflowers, rye or barley. In

'97 he added crambe to his farm for either of the swing years. The oilseed crop is better suited than canola for organic production because it is resistant to diseases and tolerant of flea beetles.

He underseeds oats or flax in Year 2 with the soil-improving clover at 10 pounds per acre. He also underseeds his Year 5 crops with the clover. Its deep rooting tendency opens subsoil macropores and brings up deep nutrients to the surface. Killing the cover crop deposits these minerals on the surface within the abundant residue, which breaks down to build soil fertility and organic matter, stimulating biological activity.

Jacobson disks down the weed-smothering, biennial legume in late June after it has overwintered then regrown to early blossom stage. The stemmy biomass breaks down through the summer fallow season as the soil also absorbs water throughout summer.

"In my rotation, I have early crops followed by late crops followed by green manure," he explains. The rotation design shifts tillage and times when soil is not covered with crops each year. "The sequence give me a whack at early

> *"Our family has chosen not to expand acreage, but instead to intensify and diversify our operation. This priority supports community and allows us to intimately know our farm."* — Terry Jacobson

weeds in the second year [after fallow] with a late-seeded crop. Then I get them all in the third year with the cover crop."

Harsh winters and a four-month growing season require spring-planted crops. Weed control, however, starts in October. "The last cultivation in fall is our first weed management for spring," Jacobson says. He uses 4-inch beavertail shovels (pointed at the bottom, wide at the top) on his **chisel plow.** The shovels leave soil roughly ridged with some incorporation of residue. The pass exposes roots of fall growing weeds such as quackgrass and field bindweed to winter's wrath. He makes a second fall pass if weeds begin to regrow, or if quackgrass is a problem.

Jacobson sees additional benefits of the pass: over winter, ridges trap more snow and lessen wind erosion; come spring, there's faster soil warming and residue breakdown.

To stimulate weed growth, he harrows in late April as soon as soil dries out. His Herman **stiff-tine harrow** has round tines about five-sixteenths of an inch in diameter. He controls the subsequent weed flush with a **field cultivator** outfitted with 9-inch sweeps. He makes a second pass if weed pressure is heavy and if he can delay planting.

Planting is also a weeding pass. A favorite tool is his Morris Seed-Rite hoe drill. The 18-foot unit drops seed behind hoe-point openers, then runs a rod weeder over the rows about an inch below the surface. The turning rod firms in the seed, leaves a fluffy dust mulch, and spins up any weeds to dry out on top. The drill is a

good load for his Case 1070, a tractor with 108 hp. (The Seed-Rite line, with units up to 40 feet wide, was discontinued in 1990.)

"My grain comes up two to three days ahead of my neighbors," Jacobson boasts. But he's quick to admit that the newer air drills that most farmers of the area use are easier to transport, easier to load, much faster and have much larger seed tanks.

"But the drill fits my farm perfectly because I don't farm a huge farm," he explains. "I need the fast emergence and extra weeding action I get with the Seed-Rite."

Jacobson watches the seeded fields closely to determine the last possible day he can do a postplant, preemergence return trip with the Herman harrow. Set at its least aggressive angle, he pulls the drag harrow over the fields at a 45 degree angle to the rows. Tines penetrate about three-fourths inch, not threatening the seeded grain which is rooting at its planted depth of 1.5 inches. This pass knocks out small seeded weeds such as wild mustard and field pennycress—also called French weed or fanweed (*Thlaspi arvense*).

This is the final mechanical weed control he can do on his grains with his present equipment. In '96, it wasn't quite enough to prevent an economically significant amount of wild mustard from surviving a wet spring. While his stiff-tine harrow is too aggressive to pull through standing grain, he believes a lighter **flex-tine harrow** would be ideal for uprooting the next flush of mustard and French weed. Also on his wish list is a rotary hoe for controlling tiny weeds in young standing sunflowers.

The stiffer tines of his harrow don't kill the grain, but they stress the plants enough to set back maturity about a week. "With my short growing season, that's a serious issue," he explains.

Jacobson selects tall crop varieties for height to better shade out weeds. The decision is easier because some tall varieties also carry the superior milling and protein characteristics that organic millers look for in premium grains. The high-yielding semi-dwarf varieties grown around him are about 6 to 9 inches shorter.

He notes an irony. Following high yield years, his neighbors worry about how to get their straw to decompose so that it doesn't harbor crop disease organisms. "I've got lots taller stalks, but my biologically active soil means I don't have to worry about whether my straw will decompose." He explains that the robust microbial activity prevents harmful organisms from dominating and causing plant disease.

Further, he has less green foxtail (pigeon grass) and wild oats—two varieties of weeds he says are symptoms of tight, unhealthy soil—than do his neighbors. Kochia, a drought tolerant escaped ornamental crop, is showing some herbicide resistance in his area. When excess nitrogen (N) is present in soil, kochia can emerge after wheat and overtake the crop. His organic soils don't have extra N, a condition which attacks kochia at its vulnerable point, he says.

"Good soil makes a difference in weed control. My soil flows well between cultivator sweeps for good weed kill," says Jacobson. "You can walk the edges of my farm and see the lack of clods on my side of the line fences."

Other important tools include

• A Noble **wide-blade sweep plow** to manage the sweet clover residue during summer fallow. Two seven-foot blades undercut surface weeds. The flat V-blades sweep back at a slight angle from the leading center point. One or two diskings begin to cut up the residue, and coulters ahead of the Noble plow's two vertical shanks help it to move through the material without plugging.

"No weed gets past those sweeps,"Jacobson says, a trait he banked on in a recent year when a neighbor turned him in to local officials for having patches of noxious Canada thistles in a wheat field. He declined the spray order and turned to a time-tested protocol in an old USDA bulletin. "At purple bud stage, go in with the sweep plow and slice off every one of the stalks. Then work them up. After that, go back in every 21 days until frost."

• **Foot-wide sweeps** on his chisel plow. He exchanges the gouging, ridging beavertail points in favor of sweeps when he wants to attack quackgrass after wheat, or when he wants to partially incorporate especially heavy straw. The tillage starts a composting action over winter, he observes, and causes harvested weed seeds to germinate more quickly come spring.

• **Row-crop cultivator.** His eight-row, low-residue Dacron cultivator has five **S-tine shanks** working between 30-inch row spacings. Two-inch shovels vibrate actively to kill weeds. He sets the inner sweeps to run within 3 inches of the sunflower rows and uses flat **panel crop shields.** He found in the wet spring of '96 that wild mustard more than 8 inches tall had root balls that build up between and plug the close-set shanks.

He cultivates sunflowers when they are about 6 to 8 inches tall—earlier if he wasn't able to back-harrow weeds after planting. He will cultivate the crop as short as 3 inches tall if weeds threaten.

Jacobson got better weed control than the S-tines give when he used to use an old four-row **rolling cultivator.** He tilted the spider gangs to throw his free-flowing soil away from the row at first pass, then at second pass to kick soil back into the row areas to smother in-row weeds. He's not able to move soil with his wider, faster S-tine unit. But the narrower implement had its drawbacks. "The rolling cultivator has to be set so precisely, and you have to maintain two bearings on each spider gang," he recalls.

Part of the problem, he admits, is that row crops just don't seem natural to him, even though sunflowers are his best commercial crop. But seeing soil between rows of crops instead of a solid crop is a practice his family and neighbors still regard with lingering suspicion. "I hate every minute in row crops. It's just not something we've associated with 'farming' in this area."

Any tool requires an operator who sees the big picture of the farm and has the interest and desire to make the tool work within its capabilities. Jacobson is willing to do that adapting when it fits within his time constraints and his goals of building soil, profitability and long-term ecological sustainability.

Toward that end, he intentionally cultivates more slowly than he could, keeping speed down to 5.5 mph—even 5 mph when he's he feeling most disciplined. "Tillage for weed control is a necessary evil. I do as little damage to soil structure as I can and try to do as much in other ways to enhance soil health as a good defense against weeds getting started." ∎

Oregon's deep soils, sloping fields reward gentle, careful tool use

Clinton Reeder
Pendleton, Oregon
• *1,400 acres wheat* • *mulch tillage* • *deep silt-loam soils with enough clay to crust* • *75 percent of land with slopes 2 to 8 percent; balance steeper* • *10 to 22 inches precipitation, depending on field location* • *wheat-fallow two-year sequence, with a rotating quarter of the land cropped annually in barley, canola, mustard or cannery peas*

Weed management highlights
Strategies: Minimum tillage... careful match of weed tools with soil conditions... hand roguing

Tools: spring-tooth harrow... spike-tooth harrow... rod weeder... chisel plow... tandem disk.... rod-tine-sweep combination

In Clint Reeder's part of northern central Oregon, the Blue Mountains have a lot to do with how farmers farm and control weeds.

"You lose a half-inch of rainfall per year for every mile you are away from the mountains," he explains. "In close, you can raise annual crops. My area is a wheat-fallow rotation, because we have to wait for a year between crops for enough moisture to plant."

This is the Columbia Plateau, a vast region of rolling hills and variable soils in central Oregon and Washington. Because he has deep topsoil that retains water well, Reeder can manage residue and tillage to produce a good wheat crop (85-95 bushels per acre) on the alternate production years. Shallower soils in the region lose as much moisture as they gain each year, requiring different techniques.

"I'm committed to relying as heavily as we can on mechanical tillage, then using the fewest, safest herbicides we can to maintain production," says Reeder. A no-herbicide wheat crop isn't in his plan, but he knows its limits in his two-year, wheat-fallow system. In '95 he raised 1,000 acres of herbicide-free wheat. "First time. Last time," is the way he sums up the experience.

He had burned residue in '93 to control disease on those same acres. The fire cleaned up broadleaves and cheatgrass, but seemed to open a niche for tarweed fiddleneck (*Amsinckia lycopsoides*), a tough-stemmed, bristly annual. It invaded in patches where there had been annual crops or an area of freezeout within the previous 15 years. His yield was 17 bushels per acre lower where the tarweed was bad, compared with 95 bushels per acre where weeds were under control.

His other weed challengers are various thistles that germinate year-round and the cool-season pests of cheatgrass, goatgrass and wild mustard. He's battling field bindweed in one 160-acre field that has enough moisture for continuous annual cropping. He rotates in cannery peas, canola or culinary mustard, seeking to use differences in soil cover and root structure to weaken the bindweed patches.

The fallow-season schedule fluctuates with moisture conditions, but field work follows in a general progression after harvest in July or August. Reeder controls weeds in the stubble by using a **tandem disk** or **field cultivator** in the fall. When he notes random escaped weeds that could cause a problem, he uses a sharp hand hoe.

He **chisel plows** with **wide sweeps** as soon as he can in February or March. The pass controls winter-annual weeds while maintaining 80 to 90 percent of the residue, and opens the soil to receive the spring rains.

The combination of residue levels, soil condition, and surface moisture determines which tools he uses before and after applying fertilizer in April or May. Options include a field cultivator, **rod weeder,** springtooth harrow or a combination tool (Culta-Weeder, below) that is heavier but able to combine more treatments with one pass. Reeder's rule is to do tillage as shallowly, as infrequently and with as little soil impact as possible—while still allowing moisture to soak in.

He drills in wheat from mid-September through the third week of October as his varied soils reach the right moisture conditions. He usually applies a herbicide treatment in some parts of his fields about March. Rate and material depends on which weeds hit an economic threshold.

He makes the most of the flexibility of the three-way action of the Calkins Culta-Weeder. The trailer-mounted, secondary tillage tool works well for him in many fallow situations. It displaces, uproots, and pulls out weeds, then leaves them exposed to dry.

The frame resembles the structure and strength of a chisel plow. His model has three 12-foot sections, with the two outer wings folding up for transport. Two ranks of C-shanks with sweeps open soil of the weed root zone. A third toolbar is the mounting point for rod weeder sections and **flex-tine harrow** sections.

"The Culta-Weeder loosens up the soil, kills weeds and levels soil for planting," says Reeder. Considering its multiple roles and mobility, Reeder feels the $23,800 tool pays its way. He's careful to keep it off moist soil, though, to avoid wheeltrack compaction that can channel water and allow soil erosion. Later in the season, soil is firm enough and the rainfall light enough that the tool's action poses little erosion risk, even on his sloping ground.

He can tailor the tool's soil impact by ground speed, adjusting any one of the three components, by disengaging one of the components, or by dropping the hitch height to change the depth alignment. Other adjustments include

Shanks. Reeder usually wants just enough tillage to improve water infiltration. He runs 6-inch duckfoot sweeps on 12-inch centers, leaving half the surface undisturbed. Depth of the sweeps helps to keep the depth of the rod weeder consistent. If soil is loose and dry, he may flip up the shanks for no sweep action.

Rod weeder. This 1-inch square rod spanning each 12-foot section is the main weed-killing part of the tool. A ground-drive mechanism spins the rod so that the leading edge is moving upward, ripping up weeds and flipping them onto the soil surface. Reeder drops the depth as low as 2.5 inches when weeds are tall (8 inches), but usually runs it at about 1 inch.

Flex tines. "The tines give you a compromise between soil structure and weed kill," Reeder explains. "A flatter angle is less aggressive, just right for small weeds when soil isn't crusted. As you stand the tines up, you cover wheel tracks better and kill bigger weeds, but sometimes beat up too much on the soil."

When the Culta-Weeder's combinations aren't right or its weight (9,000 lbs.) is too heavy for conditions, Reeder selects a simpler and lighter tool.

Reeder's lowest impact tools are a springtooth harrow or simple rod weeder. Both tools are good at plucking weeds—the springtooth up to 3 inches, the rod weeder up to 8 inches—and leaving them on top to dry out.

The classic springteeth are made of flat spring steel used in an upside-down C-shape. They are fastened to a light toolbar at the front. The pointed tips vibrate in all directions just below the surface in loosened soil but accommodate only minimal residue without bunching it up. Their low draft enables Reeder to pull a 60-foot springtooth with the same 235-hp tractor needed to pull the 36-foot Culta Weeder. He often uses the harrow on soft, recently plowed soil.

When he needs only weed control in a field with good residue, his standard rod weeder is the tool of choice. It's light and runs quickly through fallow fields. Reeder values and carefully manages the tool's second benefit—the thin compaction layer formed at its bottom surface by the turning motion.

"Creating a moisture barrier with the rod pan is critical in this dry country," Reeder has found. He avoids setting the layer too early in spring where it could prevent rainfall from penetrating, thus causing erosion.

Whenever possible he runs the rod weeder about 2.5 inches deep after the final rain of early summer. This pass takes out weeds and stops moisture from escaping. The layer stops capillary action of moisture moving from subsoil to the surface. Moisture stays below the line, and the "dust mulch" of loose soil and residue prevents evaporation. He continues to use the rod weeder or harrow at a shallower level throughout the summer fallow season until fall planting.

Reeder grapples with tradeoffs from higher residue in his fields. He wants to keep protecting soil and smothering weeds, but high-moisture years bring bigger wheat stalks and more straw. He likes the yield, but has to deal with greater disease potential from fungi that thrive in moist, dead vegetation.

Further, bringing more precipitation into the soil increases leaching of toxic soluble salts from deep subsoils into groundwater. This phenomenon has caused pH to shoot up to 9.4 in one low area of his farm. He accepts these challenges as part of learning a more sustainable system on his side of the Blue Mountains. ■

Innovator adds new summer crop to suppress troublesome goatgrass

Grant Smith
Lehi, Utah
• *11,000 acres, flat land* • *hard red winter wheat, safflower*
• *fallow system on mulch-till land* • *soil types: clay-loam; some sandy clay-loam* • *12 inches annual precip.; 6- to 18-inch variation, mostly spring* • *weeds: jointed goatgrass, Russian thistle, wild shiny lettuce*

Weed management highlights
Strategies: fallow cultivation... crop rotation with summer annual
Tools: chisel plow... tandem disk... rod weeder

Jointed goatgrass, like the tares of Biblical times, grows right up with a wheat crop. Seeds from the tenacious invader traveled with seed wheat for several seasons in the 1980s before northern Utah farmers realized they had a serious threat in their fields.

During the same time, Grant Smith joined many ranchers in experimenting with no-till wheat. They wanted to till the soil less, squeeze in an extra crop with less land in fallow, and make a little more profit.

They hoped to find a management option in a dryland farming situation that presents them with few other cropping alternatives. But surging goatgrass and declining rainfall combined to confound the plan and spurred Smith to look for a new spring crop. Since the new grass weed has become established, mechanical tillage is again a necessity. "If I use no-till every year, the goatgrass population explodes. So we're working to keep it down."

Researchers say as few as two plants of the grass per square foot can reduce yields of winter wheat by 30 percent. Each plant can produce from 80 to 600 seeds, with the final 1 percent of seeds staying viable through the fifth year in the soil.

Even before goatgrass arrived, one of Smith's favored techniques was to plant barley as a weed-fighting rotation crop. The spring-planted grain followed wheat, which he harvests in July or August. About half the time, post-harvest weed pressure in wheat is intense enough to require a pass with his 48-foot **chisel plow.** Excess stubble and volunteer wheat seedlings can also prompt the cultivation. He uses 2-inch straight points on 12-inch centers to create a rough, snow-trapping surface.

When he plants a summer crop, he chops up the first flush or two of weeds with his 33-foot **tandem disk.** The disk's smooth, 24-inch blades on 9.25-inch spacing are effective in dealing with heavy residue or large weeds.

He starts weed-controlling tillage as early as possible in March and April. His goal is to clean the fields, incorporate residue and open up the soil to capture anticipated spring rains. As soon as a seedbed is ready with sufficient moisture, he plants.

To pay its way, barley needs the equivalent of at least several inches of rain—stored in the soil or fresh from the sky—by the time it reaches boot stage in mid-June. Summers with barley-safe moisture levels began tapering off about a decade ago, just as the goatgrass began take up residence.

So he tried a new summer crop that would compete with the goatgrass and allow fall tillage to knock out the weed's new seedlings. Smith pioneered the use in Utah of safflower, an oilseed, as a more drought-tolerant summer crop. The plant resembles a small, bushy sunflower with a yellow blossom, prickly stems and a vigorous taproot system.

Following a final light disking, Smith drills in safflower. After trying many rates both higher and lower, he says 25 pounds of seed per acre gives the most dependable, cost-effective stand. If weed pressure is high, he uses a pre-plant incorporated broad spectrum herbicide.

Safflower develops slowly at first, when weed control is most critical. Its bushy leaves provide late-season weed control. The final result is usually weed pressure similar to wheat, he says, but with a suppression effect on goatgrass.

He uses the wheat head on his combine to harvest safflower in October and hopes for a yield of 1,000 pounds per acre. Net profit per acre is a bit lower than for wheat, but the second crop serves a valuable weed-fighting role. He rotates the summer annual break in the wheat-fallow-wheat rotation to all his fields. He treats the harvested safflower fields the same as wheat lands, tilling just enough to control weeds through the following winter and summer fallow seasons.

He's also used herbicides to control weeds on summer fallow. The practice preserves enough moisture to allow him to skip the fallow season in alternate years when there is sufficient soil moisture.

"You can get an extra crop, but yield drops," he says. He's waiting for wetter fall seasons and good weed control before trying back-to-back wheat again. Smith manages about half of his acreage—"the better land"—in a wheat-safflower-fallow rotation, with the balance in wheat-fallow.

Fallow weed management starts in April with the chisel plow. This time he outfits it with 16-inch sweeps on the curved, solid shanks that run 1 foot apart. He runs the sweeps 4 to 6 inches deep, the same depth as the fall passes with the chisel points.

"I travel about six miles per hour when I'm chiseling. No faster," says Smith. "Higher speed makes the sweeps harder to keep in the ground and harder to drive straight. Plus it's harder on equipment."

He comes back to the fallow fields with the tool when weeds rebound in June, then again in late August or early September. Some seasons take as many as four passes. Smith knocks down the weeds while keeping all the residue he can on the surface. He raises the sweeps about an inch each time to bring the subsoil moisture zone closer to the surface in anticipation of fall wheat planting.

He runs his 64-foot Leon **rod weeder** if he needs a final pre-plant weeding pass. The implement is a ground-driven model with a round rod that spins just beneath the soil surface. Smith feels the square rod used in the 1930s did a better job of weeding. Maintenance of drive sprockets and chains is important, he says, as is keeping speed below 4 mph to prolong tool life and avoid downtime.

Smith approached his 1997 season with confidence that he has a good weed management system in place. He feels it's one that will work just as well when "normal" precipitation returns as it has during the past seven years of drought. But like other good farmers, he's still looking for better ways to hold back weeds and give his crops the advantage. ∎

TOOLSHED

Farmer Sidebars

Gary Thacker

Precision guidance technology can pay its way

Guidance systems that automatically keep cultivators the desired distance from the row greatly relieve operator stress, according to many farmers who use them. Extension Agent Gary Thacker's recent work—as well as agricultural engineer Richard Parish's several years of experience with bedded vegetable crops in Louisiana—show efficiency benefits clustered around greater speed and accuracy.

• **Faster cultivating speed** reduces labor expense and increases acres covered per day with the same equipment.

• **Greater precision** widens the inter-row area dependably covered by mechanical weed control and reduces the width of the herbicide band over the row. This cuts chemical cost and use per acre.

• **Standardizing width** between the outside rows of successive passes nearly eliminates width variance in guess rows. This makes mechanical weed control possible without extra effort for the irregularly spaced rows, and allows the interchangeable use of six-row and four-row equipment in the same field.

Overall, both researchers found that the higher productivity achieved with the guidance systems offsets added costs of the tools in their crop systems.

See: Guidance Systems, page 30.

Dick and Sharon Thompson

Fit cover crops to *your* farm

The more crops you rotate, the more decisions you have for cover-crop management. Whether you're finding or refining your system, try the checkpoints Iowa farmers Dick and Sharon Thompson use in their search for efficient sustainability:

• **Weigh the costs** (in labor, expense and possible moisture loss) **and benefits** (fertility, soil quality and nutrient management, as well as weed control).

• **Evaluate:** rotation niches; broadcast or drilled establishment; legume or grass species, to respectively fix or recycle nitrogen; and mowing or tillage (or herbicides, if you use them) to kill the covers.

• **Determine** the most desirable biomass volume and synchronize its arrival with your planting cycle.

While few farmers have the inclination to record data as extensively as do the Thompsons, casually "trying" a cover crop or other weed-control practice often yields inconclusive results. The Thompsons maximize returns from their on-farm trials by using down-time to carefully study the disciplined, timely observations they make during the crop year.

Your decision-making ability deepens with yearly additions to records on critical points in crop cycles. These include dates for **tillage, planting, germination** (weed species and crops), **spiking** through the ground, **hoeing** and **cultivation** as well as **plant population** and **weed levels** pegged to identifiable **crop stages.** These data—matched with **crop yield** and practice costs—provide revealing clues to more profitable weed management economics.

For on-farm research set-up details consult "The Paired-Comparison: A Good Design for Farmer-Managed Trials," an excellent (and free) six-page guide from Practical Farmers of Iowa, 2104 Agronomy Hall, ISU, Ames IA 50011; or *A Farmer's Guide to On-Farm Research,* an 18-page booklet that explains why and how you can gain sharper insights through replicated research.

For the Guide, send $5 to: Rodale Institute Research Publications, 611 Siegfriedale Road, Kutztown PA 19530.

See: Thompson, page 35.

Dick and Sharon Thompson

Ridge-Till Planters Suppress In-Row Weeds

Ridge-till planters do everything no-till planters do—seed a crop into previously untilled soil across many field situations. Yet ridge units can also greatly reduce weed pressure by leaving the row area free of weed seeds that will quickly germinate.

Employing either horizontal disk or sweep-type ridge cleaners, these planters skim all residue and a thin layer of soil from the ridge top. A carefully designed sequence of tooling keeps this weed-seed laden soil flowing away from the row. The remaining planting-zone soil is untilled, leaving its weed seeds below the surface largely unexposed to the light or movement that triggers germination.

By not tilling between harvest and planting,

Dick and Sharon Thompson of Boone, Iowa, keep most weed seeds dormant. Another member of the Practical Farmers of Iowa, a farmer group that conducts extensive on-farm testing of sustainable practices, recorded 90 percent fewer weeds (in-row at harvest) in ridge-till compared with conventional tillage. Thompson's tests show that any type of tillage prior to planting increases weed pressure.

A runner-type seed opener works well in the moist soil conditions he often encounters at planting. Disk openers are effective in dry, trashy conditions but plug more often in moist soil, he reports.

See: Thompson, page 36.

Rex and Glenn Spray

Disking down clover secures sloping soil

COSHOCTON, Ohio—A friable, crumbly soil structure minimizes runoff despite a relatively low residue cover, a phenomenon documented in work at the USDA-ARS hydrologic station here. The site is about 40 miles east of the Knox County farm of Rex and Glenn Spray, and used even steeper slopes for a test that verified the effectiveness of their system.

Soil scientists concluded a six-year study in 1996 that compared disked and cultivated plots with herbicide-treated plots that were chisel-plowed and no-tilled, all on steeply sloping fields. Results showed that corn yields and erosion control in their disked plots were better than or comparable to the other two systems.

The experiment used a three-year rotation of corn, soybeans and wheat/red clover. All treat-

ments received solid beef-cattle manure and only 50 pounds of actual N. Herbicides were applied at half-rate. Technicians disked the mechanical weed control plots to prepare seedbeds two out of three years, cultivated annually for weed control, and used a rotary hoe as needed to relieve soil crusting.

Soil scientist Dr. Bill Edwards, former director at the Coshocton station, commented on the study. "Light disking that incorporates the manure and red-clover sod residue into the top three inches of soil, along with the soil aggregates the clover helps to create, can produce good crops at a good profit. Our grandfathers knew how to do it. We can figure it out, too."

See: Spray, page 50.

Reviewers

Whole-book reviewers

These individuals read and commented overall on the entire book.

Jerry Doll—Extension Weed Scientist
Department of Agronomy
University of Wisconsin
Madison WI

Paul J. Jasa—Extension Engineer
Biological Systems Engineering Department
University of Nebraska
Lincoln NE

R. Ed Peachey—Weed Management Specialist
Horticulture Department
Oregon State University
Corvallis OR

Technical Reviewers

These individuals read one of the book's sections. Their comments on practical details greatly improved accuracy and inclusion of regional variations.

I. Agronomic row crop tools

David L. Carter—Soil Scientist/Agronomist (ret)
USDA-ARS, Kimberly Research Center
Kimberly ID

Rick Exner—Weed Management Specialist
Practical Farmers of Iowa
Iowa State University
Ames IA

Jim Frisch—Weed Management Tool Specialist
Department of Soil Crop and Atmospheric
    Sciences
Cornell University
Ithaca NY

Dale Kumpf—Ridge-till System Specialist
Buffalo Ridge-till Products
Fleischer Mfg. Co.
Columbus NE

John Merrill—Dairy Farmer
Stratham NH

Mark J. VanGessel—Weed Scientist
Research and Education Center
University of Delaware
Georgetown DE

II. Horticultural crop tools

Vern Grubinger—Extension; vegetable systems
The Center for Sustainable Agriculture
The University of Vermont
Brattleboro VT

Greg Hoyt—Soil Management Professor
Mountain Horticultural Crops Research and
    Extension Center
North Carolina State Uuniversity
Fletcher NC

Jim Leap—Weed Management Tool Specialist
Center for Agroecology
University of California—Santa Cruz
Santa Cruz CA

James A."Kayo" Mullins—(Director of
    Agriculture, retired, PictSweet Frozen Foods)
Bells TN

III. Dryland crop tools

Dan Ball—Asst. Weed Science Professor
Columbia Basin Experiment Center
Oregon State University
Pendleton OR

Brent Bean—Extension Agronomist
Texas A&M Research and Education Center
Amarillo TX

Robert Boettcher—Grain Farmer
Big Sandy MT

Patrick Carr—Agronomy Professor
Dickinson Research Extension Center
Dickinson ND 58601

Glossary

Definitions in current use by farmers, researchers and manufacturers or the American Society of Agricultural Engineers ((616)429-0300). See ASAE terminology bulletin on tillage implements (S414.1); soil-tool relationships (EP291.2 Dec 93) and soil-engaging components for conventional-tillage planters (S477 Dec 93).

Alabama shovels. Soil-moving sweeps in a triangular shape, 8 to 16 inches wide. Mounted on vertical or set back dog-leg shanks. A large version of a "batwing" shovel.

Barring-off disks. See "disk hillers."

Bezzerides tools. Common term for a line of in-row weeding tool sets manufactured by Bezzerides Bros. Inc. of Orosi, CA.

Blind cultivation. Killing weeds before they emerge.

Broadcast tillage cultivation. A shallow field pass treating the soil continuously within its swath, i.e., not differentiating between row and inter-row areas. Includes passes with tools like a rotary hoe, harrow or rod weeder done after crop emergence.

C-shank. A shank of flat stock bent in the shape of a "C," mounted with the open side forward. Stock is usually at least twice as wide as thick; thicknesses of 0.5 to 0.88 inch. Used for low- to moderate-residue row-crop cultivators and field cultivators.

Chisel-plow shank. A shank resembling a C-shank, but made from more rigid stock. Used for heavier cultivators and chisel plows. Usually 1.25 by 2 inches.

Cultivator. A tillage tool designed to work several inches deep to remove weeds between rows of growing crops. Usually a toolbar—attached to a tractor by a three-point hitch—is the mounting point for row units which carry soil-tilling units. Sometimes called a "plow" in the South.

Cutaway disks. Term for barring-off disks, disk hillers, weeder disks. See disk hiller.

Danish tine. See S-tine.

Delta clean knife. Wide, single-piece cultivator sweep.

Disk hillers. Disks 6 to 22 inches in diameter paired to work ahead of a cultivator gang to move soil. May be set close to row to pull soil away from small crops, or reversed (through swiveling 180 degrees or switching sides), positioned farther from the row to move soil into rows. Also called barring-off disks, cutaway disks, weeder disks.

Do-all. Generic name for several combinations of secondary tillage tools. Usually combine S-tine cultivators, harrows, disks and a leveling device, widely used in conventional tillage systems in the Mississippi Delta and central Midwest.

Drag harrow. Flex-tine harrow in North Dakota; a spike-tooth harrow in Ohio.

Drill. 1. A wheeled implement that drops grains into soil openings created by disk, shovel, coulter or power blade openings. 2. In the South, the crop row (i.e., where the drill put the seeds).

Field cultivator. Tillage tool that works 2 to 5 inches deep to open up soil or incorporate residue, depending on tooling. Sweeps often used for fallow weed control. Shovels used more for spring field prep. Designed for broadcast tillage across the entire working width. Four to five toolbars of C-shanks are common.

Flame weeder. A mounted combination of a portable fuel source and burners that generate flame hot enough to kill weeds. Tractor mounted flamers can be used broadcast to cover the entire toolbar width, or with more directed burners to work between or in rows of growing crops. Backpack type flamers cover small areas with precision manual control.

Flex-tine weeder. Light implement for broadcast tillage cultivation. Multiple round or angle iron framing members hold round or flat spring steel teeth that run up to 0.5 inches deep, vibrating and moving around obstructions. Also drag harrow (North Dakota), finger harrow, tine tooth harrow, or weeder. "Weeder harrow" usually has much thicker tines—almost spikes.

Glossary—*continued*

Gang. A single structural member, mounted at right angles to a main toolbar, that holds a grouping of cultivating tools. Usually connected to the toolbar by a parallel linkage so it follows soil contours. Also rig (John Deere) or row unit.

Guidance system. Any combination of mechanical or hydraulic parts that keep an implement oriented a set distance from the row as the implement moves down the field.

Hydraulic systems usually have sensors that use the location of the crop row or a soil formation to control adjustments to the implement's position.

Knives. Thin metal soil engaging tooling meant to slice off weeds without displacing soil.

One-piece sweep. Wide sweep used in high-residue conditions. Designed to undercut weeds and minimize surface residue incorporation. Wings extend back from raised center, with open space between for soil flow. In contrast to "three-piece sweep" which serves a similar function. Also Texas sweep.

Plowing. Cultivating weeds between rows with a shanked implement (Texas).

Point-and-share sweep. See "three-piece sweep."

Rig. Cultivator gang, the structural piece as well as the piece with all its tooling.

Rod weeder. Toolbar implement that pulls a spinning rod parallel to the toolbar beneath the soil surface. The rod uproots weeds and creates a desirable compaction layer that can serve as a moisture seal. (In some areas of the upper Midwest, a stiff-toothed weeder harrow.)

Rotary hoe. A high-speed tool designed to aerate crusted soil and to pluck tiny weed seedlings from the soil. Spider wheels with curved teeth rotate around a straight shaft. Alternate wheels are offset for maximum soil contact. High-residue models increase the offset distance to allow more residue flow.

Scuffling. Inter-row cultivation

Shank. Parts of tillage tools designed to connect soil-engaging tooling (shovels, sweeps) with the implement's frame. Shanks can be straight, C-shaped or S-shaped, depending on function. Called "standard" on John Deere products.

Share. On cultivation tools, another term for sweep.

Spike-tooth harrow. Broadcast tillage tool with horizontal rigid bars that hold square metal rods about 8 inches long, turned 45 degrees so that the corner runs forward. Also diamond spike harrow, drag harrow (in Ohio).

Spring-tooth harrow. Semi-circular, flat spring steel teeth that pull with spring action when they encounter an obstruction or rooted weed. More aggressive than spike harrow, but less aggressive than disk harrows or field cultivators. Displaced by disks and field cultivators for deeper tillage or heaver soil, but still excellent for plucking out shallow-rooted surface weeds.

Sweep. Soil-engaging part of a cultivator. Versions designed to slice through soil, cut off weeds and till soil surface.

Sweep plow. Toolbar implement of great rigidity that pulls a wide, flat blade just beneath the surface. Kills weeds without disturbing surface residue. Also blade plow, Noble blade plow, wide-blade plow, V-blade plow.

S-tine. Flat metal stock bent into an "S" shape standard to hold a cultivation sweep or shovel at the open bottom end of the "S." Lighter versions vibrate the most to shake weeds loose from soil; heavier versions can run through deeper soil or handle higher residue. Used on many tillage tools and cultivators.

Texas sweeps. See "One-piece sweep."

Three-piece sweep. Wide sweep used in high-residue conditions. Designed to undercut weeds and minimize surface residue incorporation. Two replaceable (and usually reversible) blades bolt to the shank's bottom members. A third replaceable tip or point fastens on front. In contrast to one-piece sweep which serves a similar function.

Tine. A long, thin rod of spring steel, round or flat, valued for its vibrating action in shallow cultivation.

Publications and Information

These publications cover aspects of weed control from different perspectives. Ones known to be helpful for creating applied sustainable weed management systems are often annotated.

Bugg, Robert L., "Cover crop biology: A mini-review." *Sustainable Agriculture,* Part 1 in Vol. 7, Number 4, Fall 1995, pp. 15-17; Part 2 in Vol. 8, Number 1, Winter 1996, pp.16-18. Includes weed response results in a number of cover-crop experiments.

Buhler, Douglas, et al, "Integrating Mechanical Weeding with Reduced Herbicide Use In Conservation Tillage Corn Production Systems." *Agronomy Journal*, Vol. 87: 507-512 (1995).

_____, "Interrow Cultivation to Reduce Herbicide Use in Corn following Alfalfa without Tillage." *Agronomy Journal*, Vol. 86:66-72 (1994). Three-year study showing yield increases from one and sometimes two cultivations independent of weed control impact. A third cultivation did not improve yield—and in some cases lowered yield—and was never profitable. Some studies have verified this "cultivator effect," while others have not. This study also showed that early season cultivation effectively reduced herbicide use.

_____, "Influence of Tillage Systems on Weed Population Dynamics and Management in Corn and Soybean in the Central USA." *Crop Science*, Vol. 35:1247-1257 (1995).

Burnside, Orvin C., "Weed Science—The Step Child." *Weed Technology*, Vol. 7:515-518 (1993).

Center for Sustainable Agriculture, *Vegetable Farmers and their Weed-Control Machines.* Burlington VT: University of Vermont, 1996. 75-min. color video, $10. CfSA, University of Vermont, 590 Main St., Burlington VT 05405-0059. Features on-farm footage of nine farmers describing and using their tools. Includes in-row and between-row cultivators and bed flamers, commercial and home-crafted. Highly recommended.

Conservation Technology Information Center (CTIC), 1220 Potter Drive, Room 170, West Lafayette, IN 47906-1334, (317)494-9555, fax (317)494-5969. Publishes newsletters, other materials on erosion management with a focus on no-till methods. Provides a list that estimates percentage of residue left after a tillage pass by specified implements, and by fragile and non-fragile crop types.

Davidson, J. Brownlee, *Agricultural Machinery.* New York: John Wiley & Sons, 1948 (Seventh printing). Chapter 8 covers the proliferation of cultivators popular at mid-century in the U.S. Great line drawings.

Endres, Greg, et al, "Carrington Research Extension Center 1993 Field Tour, Weed Management: Mechanical Weed Control." Carrington, N.D., North Dakota State University, NDSU-CREC, Box 219, Carrington ND 58421, (701)652-2951 fax (701)652-2055. Gives specific maturities for preemerge and postemerge treatment of 21 field crops with rotary hoe and harrow; data on rotary hoeing for small grains; tool selection criteria.

Exner, D.N., R.L. Thompson and S.N. Thompson, "Practical Experience and On-Farm Research with Weed Management in an Iowa Ridge Tillage-Based System." *Journal of Production Agriculture*, Vol. 9:439-440, 496-500 (1996).

Forcella, Frank, et al, "Application of Weed Seedbank Ecology to Low-Input Crop Management." *Ecological Applications*, Vol. 3:74-83 (1993). Study suggests that up to half of the arable fields in Minnesota have weed germination rates low enough to be controlled by mechanical means alone—at only two-thirds the cost of an all-herbicide control regime. Late planting is noted as maximizing weed control and minimizing weed/crop competition

_____, and Orvin C. Burnside, "Pest Management—Weeds," in J.L. Hatfield and D.L. Karlen, editors, *Sustainable Agriculture Systems.* Boca Raton, FL: CRC Press, Inc., 1994, pages 157-197. Explains how different tillage systems favor or discourage weed species.

Publications and Information—*continued*

Gunsolus, Jeffrey L., "Mechanical and Cultural Weed Control in Corn and Soybeans." *American Journal of Alternative Agriculture*, Vol. 5:114-119. Builds case from 35 years of research reports for integrating delayed planting, rotary hoeing, mechanical cultivating and narrow rows as suitable substitutes for herbicide control of weeds in Midwest corn and soybeans.

Kempen, Harold M., *Growers Weed Management Guide*, 2nd Ed. Fresno CA: Thomson Publications, 1993. 277 pages.

Johnson, Richard R., "Influence of No-Till on Soybean Cultural Practices." ASTA Soybean Research Conference, 1993.

Hickman, John S., "Conservation Tillage and Water Quality." Great Plains Agricultural Council, August 1994.

Kocher, Michael F., et al, "Performance Evaluation of Two Types of Implement Guidance Systems." ASAE Paper No. 94-3574, December 1994.

Lampkins, Nicholas, *Organic Farming*. Ipswich, U.K.: Farming Press, 1990. Distributed in North America by Diamond Farm Enterprises. Chapter 6, "Weed Management," is an excellent resource on weed types, explaining how to attack at a weed's weak points by using cultural practices. It gives a good review of some European vegetable weeding tools.

Lazarus, William, *Minnesota Farm Machinery Economic Cost Estimates for 1996*, document FO-6696-B. St. Paul MN.: University of Minnesota, EDS—405 Coffey Hall, St. Paul MN 55108-6068, fax (612) 625-2207, http://www.mes.umn.edu/ At website, click "crops, publications" then search for "machinery, economic." In hard copy, the document is five pages of statistics listing net cost of new implements, as well as overhead, operating, repair and fuel costs.

Macey, Anne, ed., *Organic Field Crop Handbook*. Ottawa: Canadian Organic Growers Inc., Box 6408, Station J, Ottawa ON K2A 3Y6 CANA-DA, (613)256-1848. 1992, illustrated, 194 pages. $19.95 (quantity discounts). Farmer-oriented, practical details on soil and weed management, crop rotation.

Mulder, Thomas A. and Jerry D. Doll, "Reduced Input Corn Weed Control: The Effects of Planting Date, Early Season Weed Control and Row-Crop Cultivator Selection." *Journal of Production Agriculture*, Vol. 7:256-260 (1994).

Mt. Pleasant, Jane, et al, "Cultivation Basics for Weed Control in Corn." Ithaca NY: Cornell University, 1996. Order from: Resource Center-GP, 7 Business and Technology Park, Ithaca NY 14850, (607)255-2080. $3.50 ($4.55 to Canada). Stapled, 10 pages, photos. Outline overview of issues in cultivation, herbicide and mixed systems; descriptions of six inter-row and in-row tools, Cornell field-trials of comparative systems.

Rice, E .L., "Biological Control of Weeds and Plant Diseases: Advances in Applied Allelopathy." University of Oklahoma Press, 1995. 439 pages.

Rollason, S. H., et al. "Precision Cultural System." Baton Route LA: Louisiana State University, 1997. 15-minute color video, $10 (includes postage). Hammond Research Station, Louisiana Agricultural Experiment Station, Agricultural Center. Order: LSU Ag Center Communications, 128 Knapp Hall, LSU, Baton Rouge LA 70803. Shows tool use with cone guide wheels on bedded vegetable fields: field prep, bed shaping, planting, cultivating, fertilizing.

Ross, Merrill A., and Carroll A. Lembi, *Applied Weed Science*. Minneapolis MN: Burgess Publishing Co., 1985. Good coverage of MWC tools, methods and strategies on pp. 29-61.

Snipes, Charles E., and Thomas C. Mueller, "Cotton Yield Response to Mechanical and Chemical Weed Control Systems." *Weed Science*, Vol. 40:249-254 (1992).

Stephens, L.E., "Costs and Returns for Corn /Soybean Cropping Systems." ASAE 1992.

Publications and Information—*continued*

Springman, Roger, et al, "Row Crop Cultivators for Conservation Tillage Systems." UWEX #A3483, 1989, 6pp. Good, concise summary of weed control tools and their use.

Thompson, Dick and Sharon, *Alternatives in Agriculture*, 1996 annual research report of Thompson On-Farm Research. Boone IA (2035 190th St., 50036-7423). Plastic notch bound; 124 pages, $12. The family that sets the standard for on-farm research updates their sharing with another year of insights on ridge-tilled corn, soybeans, oats and cover crops.

Unger, Paul W., editor, "Managing Agricultural Residues," Chapter 11 (pp211-244) in Wicks, Gail A., et al, *Weed Control in Conservation Tillage Systems*. Ann Arbor: Lewis Publishers, 1994.

Wicks, Gail A., et al, "Mechanical Weed Management," pp. 51-99, Chapter 4 in Smith, Albert E., ed., *Handbook of Weed Management Systems*. New York: Marcel Dekker, Inc., 1995. Good overview of North American tillage history and related cultural practices; residue charts, tool descriptions, management analysis. Strong bibliography, citing works through 1992.

Wiese, A.F., editor. "Weed Control in Limited-Tillage Systems," Number 2 in Monograph Series published by the Weed Science Society of America, 309 W. Clark St. Champaign IL 61820. Focus on herbicides, effects of limited tillage.

Wilkinson, R.E., and H.E. Jacques, *How to know the weeds*. Dubuque IA: Wm. C. Brown Co. Publishers, 1979 3rd Ed. Out of print, but excellent. Line drawings and distribution maps support clear text that includes Latin and common names, as well as regional names. Wirebound; 235 pages. Worth seeking out through used-book channels.

Horticultural tool sources

Numbers refer to specific businesses in the "Tool Sources" listing starting on page 119.

1. **Horticultural Tool Distributors—regional/national.**

These sources handle vegetable system implements, components or replacement parts: 23, 24, 32, 45, 62, 64, 79, 82, 87, 88, 98

2. **Specialty Tractors for Weed Control.**

These sources have or can refer you to new or used specialty tractors (high clearance, offset seat/engine, or open-framed tractors with rear engines), or to related parts, service and information.

Old I-H and other makes, offset frames: 12, 13

New cultivator tractors: 83

New ultra-high clearance, between row, axle-over-tractor tree nursery tractors: 98

3. These sources manufacture or distribute walk-behind tillers suitable for commercial market farms: 4, 10, 37, 39, 86

Contacts

These individuals are willing to briefly respond to specific questions in their area of knowledge, or to provide referral to others in the sustainable agriculture field.

Bellinder, Robin—mechanical weed control
Dept. of Fruit and Vegetable Science
Cornell University
164 Plant Science Bldg., Ithaca NY 14853
(607)255-7890, fx (607)255-0599
rrb3@cornell.edu

Exner, Rick—on-farm research; non-chemical
weed management
Practical Farmers of Iowa
2104 Agronomy Hall
Iowa State University
Ames IA 50011
(515)294-1923, fx (515)294-9985
dnexner@iastate.edu

Forcella, Frank—research agronomist, weed
management and mechanical control
USDA-ARS North Central Soil Conservation
Research Lab.
803 Iowa Avenue, Morris MN 56267
(320)589-3411 ext 127, fx (320)589-3787
fforcella@mail.mrsars.usda.gov

Grubinger, Vern—Extension; vegetable systems
Center for Sustainable Agriculture, UVM
157 Old Guilford Road #4
Brattleboro VT 05301-3647
(802)257-7967, fx (802)257-0112
verng@sover.net

Gunsolus, Jeff—weed scientist
Department of Agronomy and Plant Genetics
University of Minnesota, St. Paul MN 55108
(612)625-8700, fx (612)625-1268
gunso001@maroon.tc.umn.edu

Kumpf , Dale—high residue tillage tools
Buffalo Ridge-Till Products/ Fleischer Mfg. Co.
P.O. Box 848, Columbus NE 68602-0848
(402)564-3244, fx (402)564-7015

Leap, Jim—farm manager/weed tool educator
Center for Agroecology
U.C.S.C., Santa Cruz CA 95064
(408)459-3375, fx (408)459-2799
leap@zzyx.ucsc.edu

Moore, Ralph—vegetable/agronomic tools.
Market Farm Implement
257 Fawn Hollow Road, Friedens PA 15541
(814)443-1931, fx (814)445-2238

Mullins, James "Kayo" (retired)—commercial
vegetable systems
21 Franwood Cove, Jackson TN 38006
(901)664-3190

Parish, Richard—engineer, precision cultivation
Hammond Research Station
Louisiana State University
21549 Old Covington Hwy.
Hammond LA 70403
(504)543-4125, fx (504)543-4124
dparish@agctr.lsu.edu

Phatak, Sharad—no-till cotton mixed systems
Hort Dept-Coastal Plain Experiment Station
University of Georgia
P.O. Box 748, Tifton GA 31793-0748
(912)386-3901, fax (912)386-3356
phatak@tifton.cpes.peachnet.edu

Rayborn, Dan—rolling cultivator management
(See "Tool sources" list, S&D Sales)
(715)289-4866

Thompson, Dick—ridge-till, no-herbicide farming
2035-190th St., Boone IA 50036-7423
(515)432-1560

Van Gessel, Mark—integrated weed
management
Research and Education Center
University of Delaware
RD 6 Box 48, Georgetown DE 19947-3623
(302)856-7303, fx (302)856-1845

Wills, James—mechanical weed control, veg.
Ag Engineering Department
University of Tennessee
(423)974-7237, fx (423)974-4514
jwills@utkux.utcc.utk.edu

Wisian, Michael—dryland/fallow tillage tools
Bigham Brothers Inc.
705 E. Slaton Road, Lubbock TX 79404
(806)745-0384, fx (806)745-1082

Tool Sources

1 ACRA Products, L.L.C.
P.O. Box 1114
Garden City KS 67846
(800)835-9190, fx (316)275-1489
Ridge-plant components

2 AGCO
4830 River Green Parkway
Duluth GA 30136
(770)813-9200, fx (770)813-6038
www.AGCOCORP.com
White row-crop cultivator

3 Alloway Mfg.
1330 43rd St. N.W.
Fargo ND 58108
(800)289-3067, fx (701)282-7043
Row-crop cultivators

4 Ardisam Inc.
1360 First Ave.
Cumberland WI 54829
(715)822-2415, fx (715)822-4180
Walk-behind tillers

5 Artsway Mfg.
Highway 9 West
Armstrong IA 50514-0288
(712)864-3131, fx (712)864-3312
Eversman preseeder

6 Automatic Equipment Mfg. Co.
One Mill Road-Industrial Park
Pender NE 68047
(402)385-3051, fx (402)385-3360
Guidance system (The Navigator)

7 B&H Mfg., Inc.
RR1 Box 53A
Jackson MN 56143
(800)240-3288, fx (507)847-4655
Row-crop cultivators

8 Baertschi/FOBRO L.L.C.
1715 Airpark
Grand Haven MI 49417
(616)847-0300, fx (616)842-1768
Fobro brush weeders

9 Baker Mfg.
803 4th St.
Alva OK 73717
(405)327-4000, fx (405)327-5900
Cultivators, dryland tillage

10 BCS America Inc.
13601 Providence Road
Matthews NC 28105
(704)846-1040, fx (704)841-1086
Walk-behind tillers

11 BEFCO
P.O. Box 6036
Rocky Mount NC 27802-6036
(800)334-6617, fx (919)977-9718
Rotary tilling cultivators

12 *Belt & Pulley* magazine
P.O. Box 83
Nokomis IL 62075
(217)563-2523, fx (217)563-2111
Vintage tractors parts, old/new

13 Berkshire Imp. Co. Inc.
P.O. Box 237
Royal Center IN 46978
(219)643-3115, fx (219)643-4015
IH specialty tractors, parts

14 Bezzerides Bros. Inc.
P.O. Box 211
Orosi CA 93647
(209)528-3011, fx (209)528-9343
In-row weeding tools, guidance

15 Bigham Brothers Inc.
705 E. Slaton Road
Lubbock TX 79452
(806)745-0384, fx (806)745-1082
bigham_bros@compuserve.com
Cultivators, tillage implements

16 Brillion Iron Works
200 Park Ave
Brillion WI 54110
(414)756-3720, fx(414)456-3409
Cultivators

17 Brown Mfg. Corp.
RR 3 Box 339
Ozark AL 36360
(800)633-8909, fx (334)795-3029
Chiselvator row-crop cultivator

18 Buckeye Tractor Co.
11313 Slabtown Road
Columbus Grove OH 45830
(800)526-6791, fx (419)659-2082
Vegetable cultivators, tillage tools

19 Buddingh Weeder Co.
7015 Hammond Ave.
Dutton MI 49316
(616)698-8613, fx (616)281-8544
Finger weeders; basket weeders

20 Buffalo Farm Equipment
Fleischer Mfg. Co.
P.O. Box 848
Columbus NE 68602-0848
(402)564-3244, fx (402)562-6112
Row-crop cultivators, guidance
system

21 Bush Hog Corp.
2501 Griffin Ave
Selma AL 36702-1039
(334)872-6261, fx (334)872-6262
Lilliston rolling cultivator

22 Calkins Farm Equipment
Coombs Mfg.
7106 W. Warehouse
Spokane WA 99204
(509)456-8552, fx (509)456-8559
Dryland tillage tools

23 Center Tractor (stores
nationwide)
P.O. Box 3330
Des Moines IA 50316
(800)247-7508, fx (800)433-1209
Vegetable tools (small scale)

24 Chauncey Farms
RR2 Box 108
Antrim NH 03440
(603)588-2857, fx (603)588-3573
Horticultural implements

25 Dawn Equipment Co.
P.O. Box 497
Sycamore IL 60178-0497
(815)756-1801, fx (815)899-3663
Ridge-till planter attachments

26 Deere & Co.
John Deere Road
Moline IL 61265
(515)289-1350, fx (515)289-3042
Cultivators, tillage implements

Tool Sources—*continued*

27 Dickey Machine Works
P.O. Box 5610
Pine Bluff AR 71611
(501)536-1300, fx (501)534-7980
Rolling cultivator, horticultural
   implements

28 Eden Valley Institute
6263 NCR 29
Loveland CO 80538
(970)667-6911, fx (970)663-7072
Backpack flame weeder

29 Edwards Grain Gard
P.O. Box 2181
Lethbridge AB T1J 4K7
(403)320-5585, fx (403)320-5668
Rod weeder attachment

30 Elomestari Ltd.
51900 Juva Finland
Partala FIN
(011)358-15-452-494,
fx (011)358-15-452-492
petri.leinonen@helsinki.fi
Brush hoes, flamers

31 Ferguson Mfg. Co. Inc.
P.O. Box 1098
Suffolk VA 23434
(757) 539-3409, fx (757) 934-3612
Rotary tillers

32 Ferrari Tractor CIE
P.O. Box 1045
Gridley CA 95948
(916)846-6401, fx (916)846-0390
Imported horticultural tools

33 Flame Engineering
P.O. Box 577
La Crosse KS 67548
(800)255-2469, fx (913)222-3619
Flaming supplies

34 Flexi-Coil Inc.
P.O. Box 1928
Saskatoon SASK S7K 3S5
(306)934-3500, fx (306)664-7672
Dryland tillage implements

35 FSH Inc.
PO Box 654
Henderson NE 68371
(402)723-4468
Mechanical ridge guidance system

36 Fuerst
1020 S. Sangamon Ave.
Gibson City, IL 60936
(800)435-9630, fx (217)784-4326
Chain "butterfly tire" harrows

37 Garden Way Inc.
1 Garden Way
Rensselaer NY 12144
(518)391-7089
Troy-Bilt walk-behind tillers

38 Gearmore Inc.
2260 Pomona
Pomona CA 91768
(909)620-6061, fx (909)620-1001
Vineyard equipment

39 Goldoni Professional U.S.A.
1163 Sylvan Shores Drive
South Vienna OH 45369
(614)852-9733
Walk-behind tillers

40 Green Hoe Co. Inc.
P.O. Box 82
Portland NY 14769
(716)792-9433
Vineyard orchard implements

41 Hawkins Mfg. Co.
2120 E. 4th Ave.
Holdredge NE 68949
(308)995-4446, fx (308)995-4315
Ridge-till planter conversion kits

42 Heintzman Farms
RR 2 Box 265
Onaka SD 57466
(800)333-5813, fx (605)447-5855
Rotary hoe accessories

43 Hiniker Co.
P.O. Box 3407
Mankato MN 560023407
(507)625-6621, fx (507)625-5883
Cultivators

44 HR Mfg. Co.
RD 1 Box 71
Pender NE 68074
(402)385-3220
Guidance system

45 HWE Ag Technologies Ltd.
B.P. 1515 Cdn.
Embrun ON K0A 1W0
(613)443-3386, fx (613)443-3386
Euro flamers, Einbock weeders

46 J.E. Love Co
P.O. Box 188
Garfield WA 99130
(509)635-1321, fx (509)635-1434
Disk cultivator

47 JI Case Co.
700 State St.
Racine WI 53404
(414)636-6953, fx (414)636-6272
Case IH cultivator, tillage tools

48 Kelley Manufacturing Co
P.O. Drawer 1467
Tifton GA 31793-1467
(912)382-9393, fx (912)382-5259
Strip-till planter, rotary cultivator

49 Kent Mg. Co. Inc.
P.O. Box 126
Tipton KS 67485
(913)373-4145
Dryland implements

50 Kimco Mfg.
9200 W. Barstow Ave.
Fresno CA 93722
(800)356-9641, fx (209)277-9358
In-row vineyard weeder

51 Kinze Mfg. Inc.
I-80 at Exit 216
Williamsburg IA 52361-0806
(319)668-1300, fx (319)668-1328
Row-crop cultivator, planters

52 Kongskilde Ltd.
231 Thames Road
Exeter ON N0M 153
(519)235-0840, fx (519)235-2931
Cultivators, tillage tools

53 Kovar Sales Co.
909 South St.
Anoka, MN 55303
(612)421-4047, fx (612)421-0140
Harrows (spike tooth/flex tine)

54 Krause Mfg. Co.
P.O. Box 2707
Hutchison KS 67504-2707
(316)663-6161, fx (316)663-6943
Cultivators, tillage tools

55 Landoll Corp.
1700 May St.
Marysville KS 66508
(800)428-5655, fx (913)562-3240
Cultivators, tillage tools

56 Lely Corp.
P.O. Box 1060
Wilson NC 27894-1060
(919)291-7050, fx (919)291-6183

57 Leon-Ram Enterprises Inc.
135 York Road
East Yorkton SASK S3N 3Z4
(800)667-1581, fx (306)783-7278
Dryland tillage tools

58 Lincoln Creek Mfg.
RD 1 Box 41
Phillips NE 68865
(402)886-2483, fx (402)886-2274
Guidance system (The Guide)

59 Lorenz Mfg. Co.
P.O. Box 1507
Waterton SD 57201
(605)886-9596, fx (605)886-9310
Cultivators, tillage tools

60 Lucky Distributing
8111 NE Columbia Blvd.
Portland OR 97218
(800)777-5526, fx (503)252-8360
Horticultural tools, Clemens weeder

61 Lutteke Welding
56360 200th St.
Wells MN 56097
(507)553-5633
Toolbar flame weeder

62 M&W Gear
1020 S. Sangamon Ave
Gibson City IL 60936
(800)221-2855, fx (800)782-0126
Rotary hoes

**63 Machinerie Agricole
    St. Cesaire Inc.**
C.P. 399, 650 Route 112
St. Cesaire, PQ JØL ITØ
(514)469-4081, fx (514)469-3659
Euro tillage tools; Rabe Werk
  weeders

64 ManuFarm Specialties
RR1, Wheatley ON N0P 2P0
(519)825-4969, fx (519)825-9138
Replacement hoe spoons

65 Market Farm Equipment
257 Fawn Hollow Road
Friedens PA 15541
(814)443-1931, fx (814)445-2238
Vegetable tools; Williams line

66 Maschio of America Mfg.
P.O. Box 930218
Vernona WI 53593
(608)845-8088, fx (608)845-8152
Rotary tilling cultivators

67 May Wes Mfg. Co.
P.O. Box 33
Gibbon MN 55335
(507)834-6572, fx (507)834-6909
Cultivator shields

68 McConnell Mfg. Co. Inc.
P.O. Box 269
Prattsburg NY 14873
(607)522-3701, fx (607)522-4100
Cultivators, tillage implements

69 McFarlane Mfg. Co. Inc.
P.O. Box 577
Sauk City WI 53583-0577
(800)627-8569, fx (608)643-3976
Harrows

70 McKay-Empire Co.
3140 E. 65th St
Cleveland OH 44127
(216)641-2290, fx (216)441-4709
Sweeps, knives, shanks

71 Morris Industries Ltd.
2131 Airport Drive
Saskatoon SASK S7L 7E1
(306)933-8585, fx (306)933-8626
morris.ind@sk.sympatico.ca
Dryland implements

72 Multivator-Mitchell Equip. Co.
10784 Industrial Parkway
Marysville OH 43040
(614)873-4620, fx (614)873-8584
Rotary tilling cultivators

73 New Noble Services Inc.
Box 359, Nobleford AB TØL ISØ
(403)824-3711, fx (403)824-3695
Dryland implements, Noble plow

74 Nicholls Tillage Tools Inc.
312 Hereford
Sterling CO 80751
(970)522-8676
Smith fins

75 Northwest Tillers Inc.
P.O. Box 10932
Yakima WA 98909
(800)204-3122, fx (509)452-3307
Rotary tillers

76 Orthman Mfg. Co.
P.O. Box B
Lexington NE 68850
(800)658-3270, fx (308)324-5001
Row crop cultivators, tillage tools,
  guidance systems

77 Peaceful Valley Farm Supply
P.O. Box 2209
Grass Valley CA 95945
(916)272-4769, fx (916)272-4794

78 Pepin Farm Implements
Northern Wisconsin Mfg. Co.
P.O. Box 158
Pepin WI 54759
(800)637-3746, fx (715)442-4121
Cultivators, tillage tools

Tool Sources—*continued*

79 Quinstar
P.O. Box 424
Quniter KS 67752
(800)225-2740, fx (913)754-2491
Dryland tillage tools

80 Roetgers Farm Supply
565 E. 120th St.
Grant MI 49327
(616)834-7888, fx (616)834-8655
Vegetable and fruit implements

81 Roll-A-Cone Mfg. & Dist.
Box 23 R 2
Tulia TX 79088
(806)668-4722, fx (806)668-4725
Cultivators, tillage implements

82 S&D Sales
24185 45th Ave.
Cadott WI 54727
(715) 289-4866
Lilliston rolling cultivators

83 Salinas Equipment Distributors
25445 Chualar River Road
Chualar CA 93925
(800)237-4585, fx (408)679-2014
Vegetable tools

84 Saukville Tractor Corp.
P.O. Box 572
Newburg WI 53060
(414)675-6221, fx (414)675-2182
saukville@portsmouthnh.com
Cultivator tractor, implements

85 Schaffert Mfg.
RR 1 Box 157
Indianola NE 69034
(308)364-2607, fx (308)364-2410
Extra-Sweep guess-row adapter

86 Sexton, Keith
2195 250th St
Rockwell City IA 50579
(712)297-7934
Rotary hoe extender arms

87 Snapper
535 Macon Road
McDonough GA 30253
(770)954-2497
Walk-behind tillers

88 Southern Ag Equipment Inc.
2723 A County Road 1250N
Homer IL 61849-9760
(217)896-2442, fx (217)896-2149
Vegetable implements

89 Southern Ag Equipment Inc.
7302 W82nd St. #13
Lubbock TX 79424-4822
(806)866-4422, fx (806)866-9702
Vegetable implements

90 Sprayrite Mfg. Co.
P.O. Box 3269
West Helena AR 72390
(501)572-6737, fx (501)572-6730
Cultivators, mechanical guidance

91 Sukup Mfg. Co.
Box 677
Sheffield IA 50475
(515)892-4222, fx (515)892-4269
Row-crop cultivators; guidance

92 Sunco Marketing
P.O. Box 2036
North Platte NE 69103
(308)532-2146, fx (308)534-0938
Guidance system (Acura Trak)

93 Sunflower Mfg. Co.
#1 Sunflower Drive
Beloit KS 67420
(800)748-8481, fx (913)738-2406
Dryland tillage implements

94 Svensk Ekologimaskin AB
S683 93
RADA SWEDEN
(011)46-563-724-48,
fx (011)46-563-721-23
Brush weeders, flamers

95 Taylor/Pittsburgh Imp. Co.
7 Rocky Mount Road
Athens TN 37303
(423)745-3110, fx (423)744-9662
Cultivators, tillage implements

96 Tebben Mfg.
West Highway 7
Clara City MN 56222
(612)847-2200, fx (612)847-3112
Row-crop cultivators

97 TFI
RR 2 Box 273
Hector MN 55342
(612)848-6663, fx (612)848-2441
Ridge-till planter conversion kits

98 Thermal Weed Control
N1940 State Highway 93
Neillsville WI 54456
(715)743-4163, fx (715)743-2921
Toolbar flamers and supplies

99 Timm Enterprises Ltd.
P.O. Box 157
Oakville ON L6J 4Z5
(905)878-4244, fx (905)878-7888
Vegetable/nursery implements

100 W & A. Mfg. Co.
P.O. Box 5238
Pine Bluff AR 71611
(501)534-7420, fx (501)534-1310
Row-crop cultivators

101 Weed Badger
5673 SE 95 Ave.
Marion ND 58466
(800)437-3392, fx (701)778-7501
Retracting powered tree weeder

102 Wetherell Mfg. Co.
P.O. Box 188
Cleghorn IA 51014
(800)626-9504, fx (712)436-2672
Cultivators, guidance systems

103 Wil-Rich Mfg. Co.
P.O. Box 58074
Wahpeton ND 58074
(701)642-2621, fx (701)642-3372
Cultivators, tillage equipment

104 Wishek Steel Mfg. Co.
112 South 2nd St.
Wishek ND 58495
(701)452-2449, fx (701)452-4292
Disk harrows

105 Yetter Mfg. Co. Inc.
P.O. Box 358
Colchester IL 62326
(800)447-5777, fx (309)776-3222
Rotary hoes

Reader Response Form

Your Turn: Straight talk about this book

We want to know what you think about this book. Please take a few moments to complete the following evaluation. Your suggestions will help us shape future SAN publications.

About the book...

1. How did you find out about *Steel in the Field?* (Check all that apply.)
 ( ) a flyer announcing the publication of this book
 ( ) the Internet or World Wide Web
 ( ) an extension agent or other consultant
 ( ) a farmer or rancher
 ( ) a farm publication (please specify) _____
 ( ) other (please specify)_____

2. Which section(s) of the book most interested you:
 ( ) agronomic row crop tools
 ( ) horticultural tools
 ( ) dryland tools

3. Did you find the information you were looking for?
 ( ) almost all
 ( ) mostly
 ( ) somewhat
 ( ) very little
 If you answered somewhat or very little, please tell us what was missing.

 _____
 _____
 _____

4. Please rate each of the following (1 = poor, 5 = great)
 ( ) readability
 ( ) amount of information
 ( ) technical level of information
 ( ) drawings and charts
 ( ) resources for further information

5. Are you doing anything differently as a result of reading this book? If so, what?

 _____
 _____
 _____
 _____

6. What other topics would you like to see SAN cover in future books or bulletins?

 _____
 _____
 _____

About you...

7. I am a (check your primary occupation):

( ) farmer/rancher ( ) university researcher ( ) extension employee
( ) state/federal agency employee ( ) student ( ) equipment dealer/manufacturer
( ) other _____ ( ) crop consultant

8. I typically get my information about production practices from (check as many as apply):

( ) other farmers/ranchers ( ) extension or other agency personnel
( ) books ( ) the internet
( ) farm journals and newsletters ( ) other _____

9. I am from _____ (your state).

10. I primarily grow (please specify crops/livestock): _____
_____

PLEASE FOLD HERE FIRST

Thank you for taking the time to complete this survey. Please fold on dotted lines and affix top with tape.

Resources from the Sustainable Agriculture Network

SAN's print and electronic products cover a range of topics, from farmer profiles to cover crop selection to locating ag expertise in a distant state. SAN's electronic books are designed to help people find information quickly. Each comes on a 3 1/2-inch DOS diskette that includes the text and the software you'll need to easily search for, copy and/or print out key sections of text. Because every word is searchable, you can look for the precise information you need.

Managing Cover Crops Profitably is a practical, introductory guide to using cover crops to save money, prevent soil erosion and prevent pest problems. The updated and expanded second edition will be released in mid-1998. The book provides descriptions, uses and proven management strategies for a wide variety of cover crops. You'll also get an extensive list of experts willing to help get you started. Print or disk of first edition, $9.95.

The Source Book of Sustainable Agriculture is a guide to organizations and their sustainable agriculture products. It provides information on hundreds of free or moderately priced newsletters, brochures, reports, books, videos and software. Released in 1997. Print, $12.

With over 700 entries, the *Sustainable Agriculture Directory of Expertise* connects you with experts. It features researchers, farmers, ranchers, Extension personnel and consultants ready to share their knowledge. Profiles of each person help you determine where to start building bridges, asking questions and finding answers. The Directory contains seven indexes to guide you in selecting which of the 723 contacts to call first. Released in 1996. Print or disk, $18.95.

Based on interviews with more than 60 farmers in eight states, *The Real Dirt* summarizes practical methods for ecological soil, pest, disease, crop, greenhouse and livestock management. Released in 1994, *The Real Dirt* was edited by Miranda Smith and members of the Northeast Organic Farming Association and Cooperative Extension. Print only, $13.95.

Drawing on results from SARE projects throughout the U.S., *Profitable Dairy Options* is a free, eight-page publication. It includes insights on intensively managed rotational grazing, value-added dairy marketing strategies, nutrient management, feedlot-oriented systems, and a list of resources. Available in print in single copies or in quantity, or on-line at the SAN web site.

SAN On-Line

Visit SAN's web site at **http://www.ces.ncsu.edu/san/** The site lists sustainable agriculture grant opportunities, research results, events, and contact information for SAN and SARE staff. You can also order SAN publications. More than 700 individuals with an interest in some facet of sustainable agriculture participate in sanet-mg, SAN's electronic newsletter. Sign up on SAN's web site.

HOW TO ORDER

To order publications, call (802) 656-0471, e-mail **nesare@zoo.uvm.edu** or use the order form at SAN's web site **http://www.ces.ncsu.edu/san/** or send a check or purchase order to:

Sustainable Agriculture Publications
#10 Hills Building
University of Vermont
Burlington VT 05405-0082

If you write, please be sure to clearly indicate each *item* requested and the *quantity* needed, along with your mailing *address* and *telephone number*.

INDEX

Note: Bold, italic page numbers indicate feature, illustrated tool entries.